NEW LITERACIES PRACTICES

Colin Lankshear, Michele Knobel,
and Michael Peters
General Editors

Vol. 37

PETER LANG
New York • Washington, D.C./Baltimore • Bern
Frankfurt am Main • Berlin • Brussels • Vienna • Oxford

MARGARET C. HAGOOD

NEW LITERACIES PRACTICES

Designing Literacy Learning

PETER LANG
New York • Washington, D.C./Baltimore • Bern
Frankfurt am Main • Berlin • Brussels • Vienna • Oxford

Library of Congress Cataloging-in-Publication Data

New literacies practices: designing literacy learning /
edited by Margaret C. Hagood.
p. cm. — (New literacies and digital epistemologies; v. 37)
Includes bibliographical references and index.
1. Educational technology. 2. Media literacy. 3. Literacy. I. Title.
LB1028.3.H34   302.23071—dc22   2009030272
ISBN 978-1-4331-0445-9 (hardcover)
ISBN 978-1-4331-0444-2 (paperback)
ISSN 1523-9543

Bibliographic information published by **Die Deutsche Bibliothek**.
Die Deutsche Bibliothek lists this publication in the "Deutsche
Nationalbibliografie"; detailed bibliographic data is available
on the Internet at http://dnb.ddb.de/.

Cover photos of books and computer by Genevieve Hay

The paper in this book meets the guidelines for permanence and durability
of the Committee on Production Guidelines for Book Longevity
of the Council of Library Resources.

© 2009 Peter Lang Publishing, Inc., New York
29 Broadway, 18th floor, New York, NY 10006
www.peterlang.com

Printed in the United States of America

TABLE OF CONTENTS

INTRODUCTION

Designing Learning with New Literacies

MARGARET C. HAGOOD

The texts of students' lives, the contexts in which they use these texts, and the activities they engage in outside of school can no longer be ignored in classrooms. Examples of these texts include constructing and sharing 3-D Lego creations online, reading and posting comments, pictures, and videos on blogs, watching Bakugan episodes over and over on YouTube in order to recreate battle scenes with action figures, personalizing cell phones with ringtones and photo contacts, or writing a song and creating a beat with computer software to then record on a computer and upload to a music distribution site. Such literacy practices associated with text use affect students' knowledge and skills, and in turn, affect how they come at ideas and content in schools. These texts and practices are *new literacies*, which Myers (2006) described as "evolving social practices that coalesce new digital tools along with the old symbolic tools to achieve key motivating purposes for engagement in the literacy practices" (p. 62). New literacies include not only technical tools but also a different mindset that emphasizes cultural and social relations that stem from valuing participation, collaboration, dispersion, and distributed expertise of literacy practices (Lankshear & Knobel, 2006). New literacies consist of several characteristics: (1) multimodalities, which include linguistic as well as visual, gestural, and auditory texts, (2) situated social practices, which are culturally, linguistically, and textually based, and (3) identities, which connect text users to text uses.

New literacies have been researched in a variety of settings with a variety of age groups, illustrating how text uses differ across contexts and highlighting stark divides between schooled and out-of-school literacies (e.g., Knobel, 1999;

Marsh, 2005; O'Brien, 2001). Not surprisingly, schools have had difficulty staying abreast of the technological and social aspects associated with new literacies. Lankshear and Knobel (2006) explained

> We are presently at a point in the historical-cultural development of literacy where we don't really know how to deal educationally with these new literacies. What seems to be happening is that the day-to-day business of school is still dominated by conventional literacies, and engagement with the 'new' literacies is largely confined to learners' lives in spaces outside of schools and other formal educational settings. Insofar as schools try to get to grips with the changing world of literacy and technology (often seen in terms of using computers in the production of texts and textual representations), they often simply end up reproducing conventional literacies through their uses of new technologies. (p. 30)

New Literacies Practices: Designing Literacy Learning takes into account these two concerns—the dichotomy of contextual uses of new literacies across spaces and concerns that schooled instructional attempts with new literacies reify conventional literacy practices. Authors in this volume are classroom teachers and researchers who begin from a stance that in an interconnected, multimodal world, new literacies exist across spaces. It is no longer appropriate to consider *if* literacies between contexts, such as out-of-school and in-school, dovetail. Instead, we must shape examinations according to *how* they dovetail. Authors in this volume forge the amorphous divide between out-of-school and in-school literacies through a design of pedagogy and examine how teachers and researchers collaborate to design instruction that accounts for students' new literacies. The studies in this text acknowledge that new literacies must be embedded into the curriculum, not just included as an add-on course or activity to the school day (Hagood, 2007; Knobel & Lankshear, 2007).

Jewitt (2008) described design as "how people make use of the resources that are available at a given moment in a specific communicational environment to realize their interests as sign makers" (p. 252). Within each of the chapters authors show how the design process of working with new literacies holds potential for shaping literacy pedagogy so that it draws on teachers' expertise, is relevant to students' lives, and recognizable within a standards-driven curriculum. To be sure, this text is not an attempt to create a new literacies instructional manual to implement in schools, which runs counter to the workings of the situated nature of new literacies. Rather, authors present exemplars of the messiness—the successes and challenges of intended and unintended consequences—of working with new literacies where many literacy practices, such as access to technology, technological glitches, and narrow views of literacy learning, defy new literacies pedagogical design.

In their theoretical manifesto, "A Pedagogy of Multiliteracies: Designing Social Futures," The New London Group (1996) noted that designers "are both inheritors of patterns and conventions of meaning and at the same time active designers in meaning" (para 15). Chapters in this book highlight how teachers and students are active participants in making and remaking texts to suit various users' purposes. They examine design processes that construct a multiplicitous view of literacy that targets the acquisition of traditional reading and writing literacies (those patterns and conventions of meaning inherited by default of schooling) in conjunction with visual and iconic texts, situated within social and collaborative practices (the parts of active design in meaning making).

Authors in this volume highlight key pedagogical components of design outlined by the New London Group (1996). These include (1) situated practice (which draws on relevant texts of users' lives), (2) overt instruction (which forms a metalanguage for understanding text uses), (3) critical framing (which develops understandings of text meanings by context and purpose), and (4) transformative practice (which values remixing and reframing designs to make new uses and meanings of texts). Chapters highlight work in various learning contexts—in classrooms, in museum spaces, and in after-school settings, for example. The authors also present a spectrum of elementary, middle, and high school students and teachers. They use an array of conventional and new literacies materials and examine how these materials are manipulated and redesigned by students who take ownership of the products they create while educators guide the process and reinforce literacy practices contained therein.

Chapter Overviews

The chapters in *New Literacies Practices: Designing Literacy Learning* present an array of new literacies. The first four chapters discuss the connections of new literacies between out-of-school and in-school contexts. Michael Bitz investigates the concept of socially relevant literacy and learning using the "Tupac Effect" through two new literacies initiatives: the Comic Book Project and the Youth Music Exchange. He illustrates how these two initiatives, which differ from edutainment and are rooted in after-school education, have made inroads into schools and begun to link new literacies associated with music and comic design with conventional literacies. Amy Johnson and Achariya Rezak present an instructional design for the development of critical media literacy pedagogy through an analysis of *Pancake Mountain*, a children's television show that illustrates how children can participate in creating media texts using a do-it-yourself (DIY) ethos and practices associated with punk culture. They describe how teachers can use this kind of text to design pedagogy about media production, critical consumption, and connections to childhood identities. Barbara Guzzetti follows up on the theme of DIY and indie (independent) media and details a variety of new literacies adolescents use to represent their identities. She examines DIY literacies of zines, modding, filmmaking, indie music, and virtual life and argues that educators' study of these literacies holds potential for appreciating adolescents' lives and a DIY ethos in schools. Jonathan Eakle examines new literacies in a variety of museum spaces and with artists, drawing on connections between multimodal texts and identities. He shows the reciprocal learning potential between museums and schools and illustrates how teachers have designed instruction that connects new literacies of multimodal texts with classroom learning.

The authors in the following five chapters examine the design of pedagogy including new literacies in schools. Melissa Venters explores adolescents' interests in social networking and blogging. She connects this new literacy practice in an eighth grade interdisciplinary unit on the historical fiction novel *Day of Tears* (Lester, 2004) to cover the topics of the Civil War and issues of slavery. Emily Skinner and Melanie Lichtenstein examine new literacies practices and culturally relevant pedagogies in their design of instruction using digital storytelling that centers on the 2008 U.S. presidential election. They analyze how the teacher addressed the intersection of students' cultural identities, foundational literacies, and new literacies while facilitating students' critical literacies and political consciousness in their construction of digital stories related to issues such as abortion and immigration relevant to students' lives. Drawing on two years of fieldwork, Jennifer Rowsell presents pictures of adolescents' artifactual worlds to offer new ways of mediating literacy as the written word with literacy as design. She illustrates how the materiality of students' artifacts has deep consequences and significance for students' sense of self. She argues for instructional design of artifactual English that builds on competencies and connects to literacies often thought irrelevant to these students in English classes. Mary Provost and Andrea Babkie explore the challenges and opportunities of coupling new literacies with successful strategies used in special education, especially those appropriate for students with mild disabilities. After tracing similarities between new literacies and strategies developed for students in special education, they demonstrate how a middle grades special education teacher designed a unit of study on Black History built on an ethos of participatory, collaborative, and distributed learning in a self-contained class, infusing new literacies into special education strategies. Finally, Paula Egelson documents the journey of four middle school teachers who successfully implemented new literacies into their various content areas based upon two schools' participation in a two-year professional development intervention of new literacies in social studies and English/language arts classes. She shows how understandings of theoretical frameworks, effective instructional, and curricula infused with new literacies contribute to positive outcomes of design.

For Further Consideration

Marshall (2009) problematizes the relationship between new literacies and current school culture, noting that "our research in new literacy studies will continue to grow, of course, but we have to ask how such research will become relevant and useful to teachers working in environments where test-driven priorities are increasingly dominant" (p. 123). Chapters in this text present a realistic accounting of using new literacies in instructional design within schools where standards and standardized testings are mainstays of the curriculum. My hope is that this text begins to show the relevancy of new literacies research in schools through movements in traditional school cultures to experiment with new literacies in the work of pedagogical design. No doubt more movement is needed, but the contributors to this book have begun that difficult work.

References

Hagood, M. C. (2007). Linking popular culture to literacy learning and teaching in the 21st century. In B. Guzzetti (Ed.), *Literacy for the new millennium: Adolescent literacy* (Vol. 3), (pp. 223-238). Westport, CT: Praeger.

Jewitt, C. (2008). Multimodality and literacy in school classrooms. *Review of Research in Education, 32*, 241-267.

Knobel, M. (1999). *Everyday literacies: Students, discourses, and social practices.* New York: Peter Lang.

Knobel, M., & Lankshear, C. (2007). Sampling 'the new' in new literacies. In M. Knobel & C. Lankshear (Eds.), *A new literacies sampler* (pp.1-24). New York: Peter Lang.

Lankshear, C., & Knobel, M. (2006). *New literacies: Everyday practices and classroom learning (2nd ed.).* New York: Peter Lang.

Lester, J. (2004). *Day of tears: A novel in dialogue.* New York: Hyperion Books.

Marsh, J. (Ed). (2006). *Popular culture, new media, and digital literacy in early childhood.* London: Routledge/Falmer.

Marshall, J. (2009). Divided against ourselves: Standards, assessments, and adolescent literacy. In L. Christenbury, R. Bomer, & P. Smagorinsky (Eds.), *Handbook of adolescent literacy research* (pp. 113-125). New York: Guilford Press.

Myers, J. (2006). Literacy practices and digital literacies: A commentary on Swenson, Rozema, Young, McGrail, and Whitin. *Contemporary issues in technology and teacher education.* Available: http://www.citejournal.org/v16/iss1/languagearts/article5.cfm

New London Group. (1996). A pedagogy of multiliteracies: Designing social futures, *Harvard Educational Review, 66(1),* 60-92. Available: http://wwwstatic.kern.org/filer/blogWrite44ManilaWebsite/paul/articles/A_Pedagogy_of_Multiliteracies_Designing_Social_Futures.htm

O'Brien, D. (2001, June). "At-risk" adolescents: Redefining competence through the multiliteracies of intermediality, visual arts, and representation. *Reading Online, 4(11).* Available: http://www.readingonline.org/newliteracies/lit_index.asp?HREF=/newliteracies/obrien/index.htm

CHAPTER ONE

The Tupac Effect
A Case for Socially Relevant Education

MICHAEL BITZ

On a winter day in 1998, I sat in the very last row of Baltimore's Meyerhoff Symphony Hall as 500 or so African American elementary school students filed into the plush seats. They were to experience a children's concert featuring the low brass section of the Baltimore Symphony Orchestra. Over the voluble din of the young audience, the trombone and tuba players huffed through some orchestral excerpts and arrangements of Christmas songs. At the end of the concert, the teachers reminded the children to clap, which they did while proceeding out of the hall, onto yellow buses, and back to their schools.

Upon my exit, a school administrator pulled me aside. He knew I was on the assessment team from Teachers College, Columbia University, which was hired to evaluate the academic impact of the partnership between the Baltimore Symphony Orchestra and the city's public schools. "What do you think?" he asked. I began to express my admiration for the tuba, which I was forced to play in high school. He quickly interrupted: "Not the tuba. The math scores. Are the math scores going to go up on the MSPAP next week?" The dreaded Maryland School Performance Assessment Program was soon to be administered, and the Baltimore schools were desperate to see a rise in scores on the standardized tests.

The school administrator's question was the byproduct of a phenomenon spawned by an experiment conducted by Frances Rauscher, Gordon Shaw, and Katherine Ky (1993, 1995) from the University of California. The researchers played a Mozart piano sonata for a group of college students, then compared their subsequent performance on an IQ test to that of students who had not heard the music. According to the researchers, the students who had heard the Mozart music achieved significantly higher scores on some of the test questions, specifically those related to spatial relationships. Alas, the Mozart Effect was born. The administrator who stood before me (and countless others) became convinced of a direct transfer between exposure to classical music and high academic performance.

After the concert, I visited some of the Baltimore schools whose students had attended the symphony concert. As part of the assessment, I prepared a set of questions and interviewed approximately 25 children about the experience. All of the children were aware that they had been on buses, they had sat in cushy chairs, they had seen shiny instruments. I tried to elicit what they had learned or valued from the music. Their answers included: "It was nice." "They played loud." One student noticed how the musicians' faces turned apple red when they blew into their instruments. Another student wondered if the musicians had to take time off from their jobs in order to perform in the concert.

Another student—a fourth-grader—told me the concert was "bullshit." He did not like the music at all. He said the concert was boring, and he wanted to know why it was important for his classmates and him to attend once a month. I expounded on the importance of cultural experiences and exposure to new things. Then I recalled my post-concert conversation with the school administrator. I said, "Besides, some people think that classical music will help you do better in school. It's called the Mozart Effect." The boy smiled coyly and said, "You know what they should call it? The Tupac Effect. Then I'd do better in school."

In the years that have passed since my conversation with that young student, many things have changed. Tupac Shakur is dead, for one thing. The internet became widespread. 9/11. And then again, in the realm of urban education so much has remained the same. With a handful of notable exceptions, most urban classrooms in the United States operate just as they did a century ago: a chalkboard where a smartboard should be, a nicked desk instead of a multifunction workstation, and rows of students segregated in their schools and neighborhoods by race and class. Moreover, our concept of curriculum is even dustier than the textbooks that we continue to supply. The pervasive factory model of teaching and learning treats students as receptacles for information, focusing on regurgitation instead of investigation and unthinking acceptance instead of deep inquiry. Scant rises in standardized test scores, touted as examples of improvement, only attest to our abilities to tweak the assembly line and manipulate pliable output data (see Dillon, 2005; Herszenhorn, 2005).

Our lack of success is the definitive bottom line. By all accounts, the academic performance of students in the United States consistently falls short of that of students in other developed nations (U.S. Department of Education, 2005, 2006). Nationwide, the achievement gap between racial groups persists. Making matters worse for urban areas, teachers with the least amount of experience are often provided the fewest resources for the largest classrooms with the most diverse needs. The result is the perpetuation of a decades-long slide into an abyss of mediocrity. Or worse: the Maryland Department of Education has since fought to take over Baltimore schools because of unshakable failure (Schemo, 2006). As another case, the New York City Department of Education won the distinguished Broad Prize for Urban Education in 2007, despite a greater than 50 percent high school dropout rate. Clearly, many youths are neither engaged in learning nor invested in education.

Through all this, the boy's words have stuck with me. What if, in fact, there was a Tupac Effect? What if children could explore their own interests, media, arts, cultures, identities, and beliefs as a pathway to basic academic skills—reading, writing, problem solving—and knowledge acquisition in the content areas? What if schools were to maximize social relevance so that a student's life experiences directly relate to classroom experiences and vice versa? Could the Tupac Effect represent an untapped social connection to learning and academic success?

Social Relevance in Context

The case for socially relevant education begins not with hip-hop, disco, boogie-woogie, swing, or any other popular music, art, or medium through the ages. It begins in the late nineteenth century with the philosopher and educational theorist John Dewey and his seminal text *The School and Society* (1899). Here Dewey outlined philosophical and tangible connections between schools and the communities they serve, a concept that continues to influence the community schools movement today (see Dryfoos, Quinn, & Barkin, 2005). But Dewey also advocated a connection to society inside the classroom through a child's individual course of study. From a curricular standpoint, Dewey argued for a connection between classroom activities and experiences outside of school, a concept that he first espoused in *The School Journal* (1897): "The only true education comes through the stimulation of the child's powers by the demands of the social situations in which he finds himself" (p. 77).

Dewey was not merely a theorist. He attempted to put his pragmatic values into action by establishing an experimental children's school—a self-described "laboratory" for educational ideas and methodologies. The school was centered foremost on the child's experiences; reading, writing, and arithmetic would come later, after the child had accepted the school as a haven for curiosity and personal exploration. The teaching of academic content was purposefully embedded into the context of society. Math lessons, for example, revolved around cooking and woodworking, two important skills of the day.

Dewey's model of social relevance in the curriculum did not become widespread for a variety of reasons. For one thing, Alfred Binet's intelligence test hit the United States hard. From 1906 to 1918, Henry Goddard, director of the New Jersey Home for the Education and Care of Feebleminded Children, used intelligence testing to categorize the mental abilities of children at his school. Goddard even invented a new word for the particularly feebleminded: *moron*. Through the work of Goddard and his other eugenicist colleagues like Lewis Terman (developer of the Stanford-Binet Test) and Carl Brigham (developer of the Scholastic Aptitude Test), intelligence tests quickly proliferated in mainstream schools. "Testing" as well as "teaching to the test" began then and there, and Dewey's progressive model quickly became overshadowed by testing mania, eerily similar to that which exists today.

But the main impediment to the widespread success of socially relevant curricula was that the approach just did not look and feel like schooling as most people knew it then, and as most of us know it now. With all the emphasis on children discovering themselves and the world around them, how could there be any time for fractions, compound sentences, or the carbon cycle? When would all the *real* learning occur? The critics' point, represented by Arthur Bestor's *Educational Wastelands* (1953), was driven home when the Russians launched *Sputnik* in 1957. How could American schools allow such a travesty?

The mainstream school systems that have ensued cannot be solely blamed for their own failures; persistent societal and economic inequalities bear a heavy burden (Anyon, 2005; Bastian et al., 1986; Fruchter, 2007; Gittell, 1998; Kozol, 1991, 2005; Noguera, 2003). But our education systems can be blamed for the disconnection between learning in school and experiences outside school walls, especially for youths past age nine. As an example, linguist and cultural critic Mary Louise Pratt (1996) described her preteen son Sam's love for reading baseball cards and her subsequent anger that Sam's school would not recognize his pursuit as "literary." Just as children like Sam are discovering the diversity and complexity of the world around them, the standardization of schooling bars them from any further exploration. Textbooks in school; manga out of school. "My Summer Vacation" in school; MySpace out of school. Mozart in school; Tupac out of school. The young boy in Baltimore seemed rather tickled at the thought of razing this educational paradigm that purposefully separates life from learning.

Popular culture in the classroom

In the attempt to reconnect learning and life, many educational researchers and some classroom teachers have explored how the infusion of popular culture into a classroom setting impacts student engagement and the possibilities for academic success (Alvermann, Moon, & Hagood, 1999; Alvermann & Xu, 2003; Buckingham, 1998; Dyson, 2003; Fain, 2004). The linkages between forms of popular culture and academic content appear logical. For example, a rap song contains many words, which some children can recite like bards. Teachers want children to become better readers and writers; therefore, the inclusion of a rap song, or other popular medium, in the curriculum seems perfectly legitimate. With this model in mind, our student from Baltimore would be getting exactly what he seemed to desire: listening to, reading, and reciting Tupac Shakur lyrics, perhaps like the ones from the song titled "I Don't Give a Fuck" (1991):

> I don't give a fuck.
> They done push me to the limit the more I live.
> I might blow up any minute—did it again.
> Now I'm in the back of the paddy wagon
> While this cop's bragging about the nigga he's jackin'.

It is a brave, if not foolhardy, teacher who plays this song as a tool for literacy development. Just imagine the deep waters in which an educator wades by introducing such popular media unintended for the classroom. Every curse word, every violent image, every sexually explicit connotation is grounds for concern for parents, and another lawsuit for administrators. The Chicago Board of Education learned just this in 2007 when a teacher showed the movie *Brokeback Mountain*, with explicit homosexual content, to an eighth-grade class. A $400,000 lawsuit was filed by a set of guardians who claimed that the movie caused their granddaughter severe psychological distress (*Chicago Sun-Times*, 2007).

Concerns about popular culture in the classroom derive from not only the questionable content of popular media but also the very notion of "popular." The essential concept of popular culture is that it is consumed and enjoyed by a large number of people. However, a classroom of 25 children is a very small sample. There is no saying that all, or any, of the children enjoy a particular rapper or rap music in general. These are 25 unique children with different experiences, interests, backgrounds, families, and learning needs. For a teacher to dictate to the class that Tupac Shakur is the subject of today's reading lesson because he is (or was) popular is to maintain the standardization of schooling. If only one student in the third row listens to Tupac Shakur outside of school, it is hard to argue why his music ought to be played inside the classroom.

The curse of edutainment

For many educators, "edutainment" is the solution to problematic issues related to popular culture in the classroom. These supplemental curricular packages couch academic content in entertaining formats ranging from movies to videogames to music to trading cards. For example, a company called Flocabulary (2007) presents SAT vocabulary words, Shakespearean texts, and U.S. history through original hip-hop songs. Sometimes the edutainment medium is traditional (that is, a book), but the content is entertaining. Mason Crest (2007) publishes a children's book series about hip-hop stars like 50 Cent, Snoop Dogg, and, yes, Tupac Shakur.

On the surface, edutainment might seem the embodiment of the Tupac Effect—the ultimate connection between school and life. After all, through edutainment young people might listen to rap music in school, albeit a reinterpretation of *Canterbury Tales*. They might read a book about Snoop Dogg, although not necessarily about his arrests for gun and drug possession or his trial for murder. Perhaps the social relevance proclaimed by edutainment manufacturers solves the problems of the young boy from Baltimore or any struggling student in the United States.

While it may seem cutting edge, edutainment is nothing new. For as long as there has been popular entertainment, people have attempted to transform it as a tool for imparting information or educational content. Nursery rhymes aside, one of the first examples of edutainment appeared in 1917 with the silent film *The Black Stork*, re-released in 1927 as *Are You Fit to Marry?* (Pernick, 1996). This movie was produced by Chicago physician Harry J. Haiselden, who believed to the horror of many people then and now that children with special needs should die rather than receive medical treatment. In the film, a young couple gives birth to a child with extreme physical challenges. Their doctor, played by Haiselden himself, pleads for the parents to let their child die in lieu of the horrible future surely to be faced. The mother witnesses this future in a dream sequence, which convinces her that the doctor is right. The child is left to die.

The Black Stork employed the power of film to not only influence, convince, and shock but also teach the lessons that the filmmakers intended for viewers. *The Black Stork* was not created for cinematic value; it was created to warn teenagers that they had better not marry if they know of "bad seeds" in their family histories. But instead of standing before a lectern and orating, Haiselden fashioned an engaging, and no doubt disturbing, story designed to simultaneously entertain and educate. Edutainment was born.

Haiselden did not intend *The Black Stork* for the school market although he undoubtedly would have been elated had the film found an audience there.

It was not until the 1930s that filmmakers began to produce edutainment specifically for school use. The humorous book *Mental Hygiene* (Smith, 1999) examines these short films, which covered everything from "Dating Do's and Don'ts" to the famously gory driving safety film *Highways of Agony*. Between 1945 and 1970, hundreds of edutainment films like these were shown in schools to the wide eyes and giggles of school-aged youths.

Movies may have been the first form of edutainment, but the lack of film projectors in school classrooms and private homes dictated that a different medium would bring edutainment to the forefront: comic books. In 1941, the Gilberton Company began to produce *Classic Comics*—Dickens and Melville in comic-book form. This series, which changed to *Classics Illustrated* in order to disassociate from the comics medium, began with an incarnation of Alexander Dumas's *Three Musketeers* and lasted until 1971 with a dodgy publication titled *Negro Americans: The Early Years*.

Classic Comics had two fatal flaws. The first was discerned by the notorious comics hater, Fredric Wertham, a German-born psychiatrist and author of *Seduction of the Innocent* (1954). Wertham traced all youth violence and depravity to the comic books of the day. His conviction of the link between comic books and juvenile delinquency was remarkably parallel to the crusade that Tipper Gore and her Parents Resource Music Center led against rock and roll in the 1980s, as well as arguments against videogames today.

Wertham was no fan of *Classic Comics* either. In *Seduction of the Innocent*, he wrote: "The comic books of 'classic' and 'famous authors' show our disregard for literature and the children as well" (p. 74). As much as one wants to loathe Wertham for his pompous righteousness, he was right about the disregard for literature. *Classic Comics* boiled great novels to soggy plotlines, devoid of rich language or character development. They were the first *CliffsNotes*, of which an enraged high school English teacher of mine once said, "Why not just spit on Shakespeare? Why not just spit on me?"

If the first flaw of *Classic Comics* was its butchering of literature, the second shortcoming was its bastardizing of comic books. The series featured thick, lifeless characters and dialogue that would make even the most studious student's eyes roll. The action and drama—the very essence of comic books that drew in its young, particularly male, readers—were filtered and flattened by *Classic Comics*. This deterioration of academic content combined with the distillation of popular media unmasks *Classic Comics*, and edutainment as a whole, as an inauthentic play to children's interests and superimposed identities.

There is little doubt that *Classic Comics* led some children to the original classic works; the comics even ended with a suggestion for readers to seek out the original "greats" in their school libraries. But just as many students used the series to skip the original books entirely, siphoning enough information from the comics to write a book report or pass a test. This ability of comic books to parlay basic information in a simple form has kept them a mainstay of edutainment. Beginning in the 1950s, comics legend Will Eisner worked 25 years for the Department of Defense to create comic book manuals about jeep maintenance. In fact, it seems as though the U.S. military has taken to comic book edutainment. In March 2005, the Army invited applications for the development of an original comic book series in order to influence Middle Eastern youths "to learn lessons, develop role models and improve their education" (U.S. Federal Business Opportunities, 2005).

Corporate tentacles in the classroom

Back in Baltimore, the Maryland Department of Education launched its own comic book curriculum in 2004. Partnering with Disney, school administrators distributed *Donald Duck* and *Mickey Mouse* comics along with a set of teacher lesson plans (see Maryland State Department of Education, 2008). Maryland education officials seem to have conducted little research into the comics that children currently consume—issue after issue of Japanese manga. Donald Duck may have been socially relevant 50 years ago, coinciding with the time when the state superintendent of education—an admitted *Archie* fan—was in grade school. One can imagine the reaction of my fourth-grade interviewee in Baltimore had he been handed a *Donald Duck* comic book to satisfy his call for a Tupac Effect.

The most troubling aspect of the Maryland "Comics in the Classroom" initiative is the willingness of a state department of education to get cozy with a corporate conglomerate, all in the name of socially relevant education. Examining the partnership from the Disney perspective, school classrooms are an enormous source of revenue. Even if products were to be donated, as was the case with the *Donald Duck* and *Mickey Mouse* comics, Disney would have a literally captive audience of school children ripe for branding and marketing.

Disney has been pushing edutainment into schools for over 60 years, which the company accomplishes in one of two ways. Option 1: Create an entertainment product—movie, cartoon, comic book—and then design a series of lesson plans so that teachers can use that product as a teaching tool. Option 2: Make use of a popular Disney character to teach content about an educational issue. Option 1 suddenly transforms entertainment into education. For example, the Disney Education website features a project that begins with "Part 1: Watch a Film" (Disney, 2007a). It is no surprise that the lesson plans direct the teacher to the Disney web-store, full of "world-class instructional media designed to enhance lessons and unlock students' creativity" (Disney, 2007b).

Disney's edutainment Option 2 puts a popular cartoon character into the role of teacher. The Inspector Gadget Field Trip Series, costing $649 for 25 VHS tapes (Disney, 1997), has the wacky Inspector Gadget visiting regions around the world, ostensibly teaching about those places and their cultural significance. Tape #3 about New York City explores the city's tallest buildings, including two enormous, glimmering towers that no longer exist. How would Inspector Gadget explain such a disappearance—did the gunpowder in his shoe explode again, or perhaps a giant wrecking ball emerged from under his hat?

Imagine all the ways that children could learn about New York City. Students could write a play about the origins of New Amsterdam. They could create a scientific model of the first subway system. They could have a debate about what should replace the World Trade Center and why. Instead a teacher pops in a dated video narrated by a cartoon character. Certainly, this cannot be the epitome of socially relevant education.

The Effect in Effect

If edutainment belies real social relevance, and if popular culture in the classroom causes severe psychological distress, then what are the possibilities for the Tupac Effect? In an effort to actively explore this question, I launched an initiative called the Youth Music Exchange (YME) in 2006 in partnership with a friend and colleague named Bill McKinney, an urban anthropologist at the City University of New York. The goal of YME has been to establish school-based record labels owned and managed by youths in underserved urban areas. The students would not only write and record original music through an in-school recording studio but also write a marketing plan, write a business plan, write a press release, write an executive summary, write a label biography, write lyrics, write invitations to a launch party, write a cover letter for a press kit, write in journals to reflect on their experiences, write, write, write, and write some more.

We also aimed to build mathematical skills by relating number sense, computation, and problem solving to the business plans and practices of the schools' record labels. Students were to conduct a distribution meeting in order to address the following questions:

- Of the 75 copies of the CD that you will produce, how many will each member of the record label receive?
- How many will be left?

- Of the CDs that are left, what will you do with them? Sell them for profit? Sell them to raise money for charity? Give them away as a promotion for the label?
- If you are going to sell the remaining CDs, how much will a CD cost to buy?
- How much money will you raise if you sell all the remaining CDs?
- What will you do with the profits?
- How will you assure that the profits are not mismanaged?
- Will you reinvest any of the profits to sustain the record label?

Also related to math skills, we presented students with a series of word problems related to the music business, such as: "A music company sold 10 copies of a rapper's CD, netting $100. But the rapper owned only 2% of the rights to the recording. How much did the rapper get paid?" Questions such as this required students to think about calculating percentages, but the questions also served to encourage students to consider common business models and the realities of the music business, or any business. With so many young people in poverty and their families in debt, Bill and I felt that it was important to facilitate critical thinking about money matters while fostering a sense of entrepreneurship and self-reliance.

In the process of building conventional literacy and mathematical skills, we wanted the participating students to sustain their entrepreneurial efforts by bringing a youth-generated product to the community in which it was created, thereby building social and career skills as well. Each record label would produce an original CD, create and distribute marketing materials to promote the label, and host a launch party in the school and surrounding community. We mapped out a 20-week framework that would take students from choosing a name and designing a logo for their record label in the first session to hosting the launch party and distributing the CD in the final session.

In order to structure YME, we established four departments in a school's record label: music, art, production, and marketing. The music department would recruit and develop rappers, singers, and musicians to appear on the recording. Students in the music department would focus on the music itself: the songs, lyrics, and message. The production department was responsible for rehearsing, recording, editing, and producing the songs on the recording. The art department would create the artwork and layout for the CD face and jewel-case insert. The art team also would design marketing and promotional material for the label by collaborating with the other departments. Finally, the responsibility of the marketing department was to plan and implement strategies for promoting the label in the school, in the community, and on the web; the marketing department would also help the record company become sustainable by selling the CD and planning the launch party.

Getting launched

After over a year of brainstorming, planning, drafting, and revising our ideas for YME, it was time to put the plan into action with a "pre-pilot"—a chance to see what YME could become in real time with real children at real schools. I reached out to two after-school programs in New York City that had been highly successful with another curricular project of mine, the Comic Book Project (see Bitz, 2004a, 2004b, 2006, 2008). PS 89Q is an elementary school with a predominantly Latino population in the Elmhurst neighborhood of Queens; MS 226 is a middle school with a predominantly African American student population in the South Ozone Park neighborhood of Queens. After a workshop with the after-school instructors who would mentor the students at their respective sites, we supplied the materials, equipment, and software, which we paid for out of pocket. We decided to put the structure and tools into the hands of the educators and youths themselves so that we could observe and learn from the ways in which they would mold YME to their own needs and purposes. In order to understand the potential successes and needs for improvement of our plan, we asked the participating instructors to email a weekly progress report. We also resolved to visit each of the sites every two to three weeks, an opportunity to gather observational and interview data related to the goals and expected outcomes of the project.

The two sites unfolded in rather divergent ways. At PS 89Q, a group of third-, fourth-, and fifth-graders (four girls and seven boys) met as a club every Tuesday afternoon for approximately one hour. These children volunteered to be part of the club after the site director and club instructor made announcements about YME in other club settings. Rather than forming distinct departments, the participants decided to share the various responsibilities. They voted on a name for the record label: Lil' Champs. They began to sketch a logo design, use the computer software to create beats for their songs (decidedly hip-hop in style), and write the beginnings of a marketing plan. Yet when it came time to write the lyrics for the songs, the group stalled for ideas. On a site visit, we got them moving again by encouraging the elementary schoolers to reflect on events in their lives or things that they were learning in school. Black History Month was on its way, so the students crafted a song titled "Tribute to Black History" about important African American leaders. The song can be heard at www.youthmusicexchange.org/sitenyc89.htm.

Things were not as smooth at MS 226, which had been plagued by negative press and a history of poor academic performance. Because of the need to schedule additional tutoring sessions after school, YME was pushed to Saturdays when the designated instructor was unavailable. In lieu of abandoning the project at this site, I volunteered to come in on Saturdays and oversee the club. On the first Saturday, a group of eight middle school boys, all of whom wanted to become rappers, coolly sauntered into the room and bluntly asked to know what it was that I could do for them. I said that I could help them record their music, which at least kept them from walking out the door. In a storage closet full of toilet paper and volleyballs, we set up a recording "studio" with a microphone that we hung from an art easel, cheap headphones, and an audio interface that we connected to a computer just outside the closet door.

It quickly became clear which of the boys had the skills to rap. For those who faltered at the microphone, I began to introduce the other aspects of the music business—marketing, production, management, artist development, and graphic design. One of the boys discovered in himself the ability to write crafty marketing pitches. Another realized that although he was not skilled at drawing, he did have a knack for font design and graphic layout on the computer, which he used to produce the look of the CD. One adamant student still wanted to perform on the CD recording. Instead of rapping, however, he chose to recite a poem— "Let America Be America Again" by Langston Hughes. He downloaded the poem from the internet; decided which stanzas of the lengthy poem to include in the recording; used a dictionary to learn the meanings of difficult words in the text such as "connive" and "graft"; practiced reading the poem to a background music track created by his friend; and finally recorded the poem, which can be heard at www.youthmusicexchange.org/sitenyc226.htm. Seeing this young boy engage in the project, collaborate with his peers, and along the way become a devoted fan of Harlem Renaissance poetry, I felt that I had finally discovered the essence of the Tupac Effect.

An outlet for the Effect

It is not a coincidence that YME was born in the realm of after-school education, an educational outlet that has discovered, embraced, and utilized social relevance in real and tangible ways. After-school education is based on an extraordinary paradox—learning is mandatory, but attendance is voluntary. Imagine how many children would go to school if it truly were not required. This is the conundrum faced by after-school educators every day. The children do not have to be there. After-school practitioners, therefore, have become very creative in how they attract youths to their programs and engage them in learning experiences.

To be sure, after-school is not just about basketball and double-dutch (two very important activities considering the epidemic of youth obesity). Rather, after-school education, particularly in inner cities, has become a main component of academic support in a child's life (*Afterschool Matters*, 2004; Bouie, 2007; Halpern, 2003). The after-school day begins with a period of begrudged homework help, followed by club activities not with worksheets (like school), nor with questionable curriculum (like edutainment), nor with inappropriate content (like a Lil' John music video). The learning that takes place after-school is not only child-centered but also child-driven, and the curricula are almost always socially relevant.

There are many examples of socially relevant learning through youth-generated media in the world of after-school education. The organization Listen Up! (2007) is a clearinghouse for youth-generated films produced in out-of-school contexts. Youth Radio (2007) brings children together after school to create radio stories about issues important to them. In these cases and many others, the participating youths are building basic academic skills. Children have to consider the plot of the story; draft a script; incorporate elements of tone and atmosphere; edit their writing; submit their work for peer revision; hone the characters and story development; deal with spelling and punctuation mistakes; share and discuss; present completed works. In other words, the children are meeting every state and national standard in English language arts.

Unfortunately, most policymakers in education are not paying attention. In New York City, after-school programs, though school-based, are run by an entirely separate administration and staff than the schools themselves. Schools and after-school programs are even funded and governed by distinct city agencies: schools by the Department of Education and after-school programs by the Department of Youth and Community Development. This purposeful separation of "fields" means that there is little if any connection between what happens in school and that which transpires after school. After-school practitioners are wary about making comparisons to their school-day counterparts, but the learning that takes place after school is often authentic and meaningful, and it usually relates to life in powerful ways.

While the same cannot be said for most school-day curricula, there are some schools (many, but not all, charters) that are recognizing the importance of linkages between learning and life during school hours. In fact, four schools in Indianapolis have embarked on implementing YME in classes, one as a first-period elective and another in a theater production class. Another school—Metropolitan Charter High School—has established Tuesdays and Wednesdays as "internship" days where sophomores and juniors establish a record label. With the guidance of their teacher and approval of the school director, the youths set up a recording studio in a room off the library. They are researching the tenets of marketing and drafting a plan for distribution of their CDs. They are developing a "wish list" of additional equipment, which they plan to present to community sponsors. They are planning a launch party for their CD release. They even aim to "hire" some of their schoolmates to fill the roles in which the record label seems lacking. Their story, and that of students at a trio of schools in Decatur township, are still unfolding. Four middle school after-school programs in Indianapolis are also on board, along with two in San Diego.

Conclusion

What did the Baltimore student really mean when he mentioned the Tupac Effect? Was he asking to curse in class, or was he looking for a textbook entry on his favorite rapper? Rather, I believe that he was seeking for his interests and ideas to be recognized. He was looking for the ability to reflect upon who he is, where he came from, and where he is going. Had he had the chance, he would have used his experiences as a springboard for learning, and he would have created his own media, shared it with others, and in doing so achieved important learning standards in a number of content areas. Sadly, I doubt he got the chance. I do not know where that boy, now a man, is today, but I hope that he found his way and became a successful, happy person.

In the meantime, curricular initiatives like YME highlight the connections between conventional and new literacies as well as socially relevant teaching and traditional learning standards. In the process of learning how to create music tracks with digital loops and samples, youths can read texts about media production, write journal entries about their goals and experiences, and speak and listen to each other about the components of their songs. In developing a business plan for a school's record label, youths can develop number sense, calculate ratios and percentages, and reinforce the basics of economics. An after-school punctuation club would be ludicrous, but honing the use of commas and semicolons within the design of a webpage for the record label is perfectly legitimate. In other words, creative learning and basic skill acquisition are *not* mutually exclusive. Engaging children in new literacy practices can be the very motivation for instilling the conventional literacy skills of reading, writing, listening, and speaking that our educational standards espouse as the cornerstones of communication.

As with almost any educational experience, the success of a socially relevant learning environment hinges largely on the educator. My observations of successful classrooms over the years have highlighted for me the importance of educators as instructional designers. As an instructional designer, the educator establishes a plan and structure for the lesson—designs a logo using Photoshop, creates a beat using GarageBand, develops a webpage using Dreamweaver. Yet the quality instructional designer also finds tangible pathways for traditional literacy development—write a paragraph about what your logo represents, read and analyze an article about hit song production by a famous producer, use at least two properly constructed compound sentences in the text of your webpage. Children take ownership of the media products that they create; educators guide the process and reinforce the learning skills contained therein. In this manner, the learning experience becomes collaborative rather than didactic, and the outcomes are meaningful to students, not just superintendents.

The case for socially relevant education ends here for now, but I will continue to explore the Tupac Effect as YME expands in New York City, Indianapolis, San Diego, and beyond. Of course, for a fourth-grader today, Tupac Shakur is likely as relevant as Wolfgang Amadeus Mozart. Yesterday's Tupac Effect is today's Kanye West Effect. For another student it may be the Kenny Chesney Effect or the Metallica Effect, and for another, in fact, the Mozart Effect. Social relevance is what a student deems important to him or her, not what adults or corporations try to dictate nor what popular culture or mass media try to insinuate. But for educators to ignore students' interests and identities for another year of textbook learning is to perpetuate stagnation. Only when learning and life truly connect will school have a purpose beyond gold stars, bubblegum under the seat, and a perfunctory understanding of parsed, irrelevant information.

References

Afterschool Matters. (2004). Retrieved December 6, 2008 from http://www. robertbownefoundation.org/pdf_files/afterschoolmatters_spring04.pdf.

Alvermann, D. E., & Xu, S. H. (2003). Children's everyday literacies: Intersections of popular culture and language arts instruction. *Language Arts, 81* (2), 145-54.

Alvermann, D. E., Moon, J. S., & Hagood, M. C. (1999). *Popular culture in the classroom*. Newark, DE: International Reading Association.

Anyon, J. (2005). *Radical possibilities*. New York: Routledge.

Bastian, A., Fruchter, N., Gittell, M., Greer, C., & Haskins, K. (1986). *Choosing equality: The case for democratic schooling*. Philadelphia: Temple University Press.

Bestor, A. B. (1953). *Educational wastelands*. Urbana: University of Illinois Press.

Bitz, M. (2004a). The Comic Book Project: Forging alternative pathways to literacy. *Journal of Adolescent & Adult Literacy, 47* (7), 574–586.

Bitz, M. (2004b). The Comic Book Project: The lives of urban youth. *Art Education, 57* (2), 33–39.

Bitz, M. (2006). The art of democracy/Democracy as art: Creative learning in afterschool comic book clubs. *Afterschool Matters Occasional Papers Series, 7*, (1-20).

Bitz, M. (2008). The Comic Book Project: Literacy outside (and inside) the box. In J. Flood, S. B. Heath, & D. Lapp (Eds.), *Handbook of research on teaching literacy through the communicative and visual arts* (Vol. 2) (pp. 229-236). Mahwah, NJ: Erlbaum.

Bouie, A. (2007). *After-school success: Academic enrichment strategies with urban youth*. New York: Teachers College Press.

Buckingham, D. (Ed.). (1998). *Teaching popular culture: Beyond radical pedagogy*. London: UCL Press.

Chicago Sun-Times. (2007, May 13). *Family of girl, 12, sues after 'Brokeback' shown in class*. Retrieved October 9, 2007 from http://www.suntimes. com/news/education/383097,CST-NWS-broke13.article.

Dewey, J. (1897). My pedagogic creed. *The School Journal, LIV* (3), 77-80.

Dewey, J. (1899). *The school and society*. Chicago: University of Chicago Press.

Dillon, S. (2005, Nov. 26) *Students ace state tests, but earn D's from U.S.* Retrieved December 1, 2008 from http://www.nytimes.com/2005/11/26/education/26tests.html.

Disney. (1997). *Inspector Gadget's field trip series (VHS)*.

Disney. (2007a). *Cyberlesson plan of the month*. Retrieved October 9, 2007 from http://dep.disney.go.com/educational/lessons.

Disney. (2007b). *Teacher's store*. Retrieved October 9, 2007 from http://dep.disney.go.com/educational/store.

Dryfoos, J. G., Quinn, J., & Barkin, C. (Eds.). (2005). *Community schools in action: Lessons from a decade of practice*. New York: Oxford University Press.

Dyson, A. H. (2003). *The brothers and sisters learn to write: Popular literacies in childhood and school cultures*. New York: Teachers College Press.

Fain, T. A. (2004). American popular culture: Should we integrate it into American education? *Education, 124* (4), 590-594.

Flocabulary. (2007). *Flocabulary: Hip-hop in the classroom*. Retrieved October 9, 2007 from http://www.flocabulary.com.

Fruchter, N. (2007). *Urban schools, public will: Making education work for all our children*. New York: Teachers College Press.

Gittell, M. (1998). *Strategies for school equity: Creating productive schools in a just society*. New Haven: Yale University Press.

Halpern, R. (2003). *Making play work: The promise of after-school programs for low-income children*. New York: Teachers College Press.

Herszenhorn, D. M. (2005, June 25). *State lowers passing score for a Regents math exam*. Retrieved December 1, 2008 from http://www.nytimes.com/2005/06/25/nyregion/25math.html.

Kozol, J. (1991). *Savage inequalities: Children in America's schools*. New York: Crown.

Kozol, J. (2005). *Shame of the nation: The restoration of apartheid schooling in America*. New York: Crown.

Listen Up! (2007). *Listen Up!* Retrieved October 9, 2007 from http://www.listenup.org.

Maryland State Department of Education. (2008). *Maryland comic book initiative*. Retrieved December 1, 2008 from http://www.marylandpublicschools.org/MSDE/programs/recognition-partnerships/md-comic-book.

Mason Crest. (2007). *Hip-hop: The complete series*. Retrieved October 9, 2007 from http://www.masoncrest.com/series_view.php?seriesID=66.

Noguera, P. A. (2003). *City schools and the American dream: Fulfilling the promise of public education*. New York: Teachers College Press.

Pernick, M. S. (1996). *The black stork: Eugenics and the death of "defective" babies in American medicine and motion pictures since 1915*. New York: Oxford University Press.

Pratt, M. L. (1996). Arts of the contact zone. In D. Bartholomae & A. Petroksky (Eds.), *Ways of reading* (4th ed.), (pp. 528-542). Boston: St. Martin's Press.

Rauscher, F. H., Shaw, G. L., & Ky, K. N. (1993). Music and spatial task performance. *Nature, 365,* 611.

Rauscher, F. H., Shaw, G. L., & Ky, K. N. (1995). Listening to Mozart enhances spatial-temporal reasoning: Towards a neurophysiological basis.
Neuroscience Letters, 185, 44-47.

Schemo, D. J. (2006, March 30). *Maryland acts to take over failing Baltimore
schools.* Retrieved December 1, 2008 from http://www.nytimes.com/
2006/03/30/education/30child.html.

Shakur, T. (1991). I don't give a fuck. On *2pacalypse now* [CD]. New York: In-
terscope.

Smith, K. (1999). *Mental hygiene: Better living through classroom films 1945-1970.*
New York: Blast Books.

U.S. Department of Education. (2005). *Comparative indicators of education in the
United States and other G8 countries: 2004.* Washington, DC: National Center for Education Statistics.

U.S. Department of Education. (2006). *The condition of education: 2006.* Washington, DC: National Center for Education Statistics.

U.S. Federal Business Opportunities. (2005). *Combine solicitation: U.S. Army.*
Retrieved April 3, 2005 from http://www1.eps.gov/spg/ODA/
USSOCOM/FortBraggNC/H92239-05-T0026/Combine%20Synopsis%5
FSolicitation.html.

Wertham, F. (1954). *Seduction of the innocent.* New York: Rinehart.

Youth Radio. (2007). *Youth Radio.* Retrieved October 9, 2007 from
http://www.youthradio.org.

CHAPTER TWO

"We Want Some Pancakes!"
Teaching for Critical Media Literacies with *Pancake Mountain*

AMY SUZANNE JOHNSON

& ACHARIYA TANYA REZAK

The Kings of Leon take the stage. They are a hard-driving band with a punk edge, but the effect of their stage presence is a bit different today. All of the space between the drum set and the bass player has been filled by fans, but not the usual fans: these fans are very short and very enthusiastic, many of them are under the age of ten. "You ready?" The Kings start to play. The song that they rock out on has not been dumbed-down for kids, instead, it has a hard-driving beat and funky lyrics. Instead of being turned off, the kids are rocking out to it. They drop to the floor and spin enthusiastically, hop wildly, and some of them sing along. This is part of the children's show *Pancake Mountain*, and the inclusion of children into the band's performance has a purpose.

Trier (2008a) explained "critical media literacy" as "a critical practice in which mass media become the objects that are evaluated and critiqued" (p. 424). Alvermann, Moon, & Hagood (1999) noted that the concept has emerged through interdisciplinary work that is concerned with examining how individuals' access to print and nonprint texts that are part of their everyday life enables them to construct knowledge of the world and their social, economic and political positions within it. To achieve this end, critical media literacy is concerned with "creating a community of active readers and writers who can be expected to exercise some degree of agency in deciding what textual positions they will assume or resist as they interact in complex social and cultural contexts" (Alvermann, Moon, & Hagood, 1999, p. 2).

Creating a space for youth to come together to critique media is particularly salient because of the dominance of consumer capitalism and capitalistic mass culture (Alvermann, Moon, & Hagood, 1999). Youth must "learn to question how their identities are constructed by the various forms of popular culture that they elect to take up [... so that they can] make more informed decisions about how they live their lives" (ibid., p. 4). Confronted by advertising in every kind of media, youth grow up immersed in a culture that becomes more and not less driven by commercial revenue. Critical literacy in this area will help children filter and negotiate the many demands upon their attention from large corporations that are overtly and covertly selling their products via television, the internet, the radio, toys, and even corporate-sponsored institutes of education. The children's show *Pancake Mountain* is one way for educators and youth to engage in the practice of critical media literacy—that is, for thinking and learning about media through this independent children's show that critiques the relationship between the mass media and popular kid culture, what Steinberg and Kincheloe (2004) call "kinderculture."

In this chapter, we analyze how *Pancake Mountain* can become part of a critical media literacy pedagogy for teachers' and students' exploration. *Pancake Mountain* appears on the internet and on Washington, DC, public television channel DCTV. Because *Pancake Mountain* takes on the kinderculture corporate enterprise and critiques the positioning of children as "consumers" through television shows, it is a good program for exploring critical media issues with youth. First, we explain the show and suggest ways that a teacher can become more knowledgeable about the program; then we provide a social-semiotic analysis of some elements of the show, comparing it to a popular television show, *Hannah Montana*, that is commercially produced. Through this analysis, we illustrate how the study of visual literacies, such as the viewing of *Pancake Mountain*, can help scaffold critical media literacy to students. Finally, we describe some specific engagements for students that involve *Pancake Mountain*.

Why Study Popular Television Shows?

Because the nature of television media is always changing, popular television shows provide rich pedagogical opportunities. For instance, shows such as *American Idol* have recently invited audiences to not only watch but also to take part in scripting the show itself. Such an act of collaboration is what Jenkins (2006) terms *Convergence Culture*, or the creative partnership of media companies with their audiences. "Convergence" suggests that television shows are no longer a passive medium that individuals watch in isolation, and television producers are savvy in their connections across media, such as use of blogs and websites that bring the show into other media arenas and literacy spaces. Instead, shows have become the springboard for creativity that ranges from fan participation to critical discussion to television-based pedagogy. Grassroots fan activities surrounding media-inspired creative work have resulted in the proliferation of literacies into such areas as fanfiction (Black, 2008; Thomas, 2007), and online roleplaying games in which people extemporaneously act out the parts of media figures (e.g., Thomas, 2007). This kind of creativity is encouraged by large media corporations among teen and adult audiences, but so far, participation from child audiences has been limited to the products that media companies have long provided, such as play with media-sponsored action figures. As a result, child audiences are often framed as passive recipients or "consumers" of television media.

Lately, media companies have seen the value of spreading adult-targeted media products across many platforms, such as websites, movies, merchandise, or music (Jenkins, 2006). Before such diversification was offered to adult media viewers, media companies promoted cartoons through movie and merchandise tie-ins, making children some of the first audiences of a multi-market campaigns. Child fan engagement with media in the 1970s and 1980s perhaps began with play related to action figures and sets that resembled sets from the related cartoons, but pedagogical scaffolding of this play was limited. Media company access to the internet has allowed companies to create sites with the purpose of promoting certain kinds of toys and activities, often very gender-biased like the Transformers website (http://www.hasbro.com/transformers/) and the Barbie website (http://barbie.everythinggirl.com/) (Stone, 2007). Some media companies with a more intrinsic pedagogical philosophy have made learning the purpose of their websites, notably PBS's *Sesame Street* website (http://www.sesameworkshop.org).

These examples all relate to how large media corporations attempt to involve their fanbases in an interactive engagement with their product. What happens when the fans themselves, in a response to the undeniable consumer message proliferated by these corporations, take media creation into their own hands? The result is a different kind of show and a different kind of engagement. Such engagement and convergence are particularly made visible in *Pancake Mountain*.

To understand how engagement and convergence occur within *Pancake Mountain*, we draw on social-semiotic analysis. We take our framework for a social-semiotic analysis from Kress (2003), who theorized that every media production (or text) arises from and represents social action, specifically, who acts, the purpose of their action, and the issue that the act centers upon. This analysis of text, and in our case the text of *Pancake Mountain*, situates the meaning of systems of signs (or semiotics) within social spaces, especially in the "social provenance, production, and organisation of content" (p. 84). Questions Kress poses are, who created the message? How was the message produced (or "unproduced") and conveyed? How was the message organized, and what does it mean? We define our term "unproduced" as arising from a particular social ethos of DIY (do-it-yourself) culture, one that depends upon a certain set of actions and symbols that convey meaning. We will explain it further below.

What Is Pancake Mountain?

For us, *Pancake Mountain* is one of the best children's television shows for pursuing critical interpretations of media by considering specific aspects of how convergence operates within the show's format. This children's television show created by Scott Stuckey, a former advertising executive, creatively and humorously challenges assumptions of children as "consumers" of popular culture and media.

> Launched online in the fall of 2003, the concept originated when a group of young parents who grew up on a steady diet of Fugazi, Black Flag, and the DIY ethic found themselves disenfranchised with the pandering, commercial-based television programming available to their children. A haven for creative-minded kids and adults alike and ten times more intelligent than *Sesame Street*, *Pancake Mountain* features luminaries like The Evens (Ian MacKaye's band) putting a spin on the old "a, e, i, o, u" drill in "Vowel Movement," the Fiery Furnaces and the Arcade Fire performing kid-friendly dance-along versions of their songs, and even sit-down interviews with the likes of George Clinton and Henry Rollins hosted by Rufus Leaking the sock puppet. (Tucker, 2007)

The DIY ethic has at its base the assumption that people are smart enough to create cultural objects, especially their own entertainment, from scratch. This is reflected in *Pancake Mountain's* decision to never dumb down content for the sake of children; children are given the ability and responsibility to take part in adult culture, especially in a culture of loud punk music and complex ideas. Indie music, or music produced outside of large music companies, is the focus of this show because the music is organically interwoven with the DIY ethos, originating from the same participants and sharing the same cultural values. The show includes a motley cast of characters as well as celebrity guests. Regular characters include: Rock Rogers, *Pancake Mountain* News anchorman; Captain Perfect, a navigationally-impaired super hero; Rufus Leaking, a goat sock-puppet celebrity journalist; and Garnett, whom the show terms *the coolest girl in the world*.

> Produced in Washington, DC the show is a collection of bits and skits that are mostly funny and occasionally flat-out bizarre. For filmmaker and producer Stuckey, "*Pancake Mountain*" is a response to what he views as dumbed-down children's programming made toxic by an overdose of advertising and product placement. (Heim, 2005, p. C01)

Although the show was not created to be "educational" per se but rather was created as a response to the worst of American consumerism and capitalism, we argue it can be a rich resource for teachers aiming to pursue critical media literacy issues with their students.

How Can Teachers Find out About Pancake Mountain?

For an educator unfamiliar with *Pancake Mountain*, we suggest to begin viewing clips of the show available on *Pancake Mountain's* website (www.pancakemountain.com) or on YouTube (YouTube.com). Because the show is committed to its independent status, it is not a networked accessed text. This aspect of the production of the show is explicitly by design. For, "according to creator Scott Stuckey, despite nibbles from HBO Family, Warner Brothers and other entertainment companies, the program remains a defiantly underground phenomenon, available only sporadically on public-access cable (check local listings) and DVD" (O'Sullivan, 2006, WE39).

The video clips found on the website reflect common features of the show's episodes. Each episode varies in format yet includes the following elements: celebrity interviews with Rufus Leaking (a sock puppet), dance parties with prominent indie (independent) bands (such as The Kings of Leon, Weird War, the White Stripes, etc.), *Pancake Mountain* News with anchorman Rock Rogers (a parody news report), and a Captain Perfect skit. Also available on the website are newspaper and magazine articles that have been written about the show, as well as biographical information on the show's creator and cast. From the show's website, full-length DVD versions of each of the show's episodes can be purchased.

What Can Teachers Gain from Analyses of Visual Texts?

We draw on Kress's social-semiotic analysis to determine what teachers can gain from *Pancake Mountain*. To make this approach to analyzing media texts more tangible for the reader and to illustrate the differences between forms of production, we draw on two examples. The first example comes from the Disney television series *Hannah Montana*. This clip, found on YouTube (http://www.youtube.com/ watch?v=rBjyhVzCIhw), exemplifies the qualities of a commercially produced children's show that are considered important to a large media corporation. We answer Kress's three questions as follows:

1. Who created the message? The very end of the clip shows the corporate copyright of the show's creator, Disney. This indicates that a large media corporation with enormous funding conceived of this show and filmed it in a way that reflects the social ethos of the company. It is a high-quality

and lush production. On stage, the focus of the camera is upon a young girl singer, "Hannah Montana," a fictional teenaged pop star played by Miley Cyrus, the daughter of a country singer. Hannah Montana's signature style is the product of a professional wardrobe artist, and her backing band (in camera briefly) is considerably older, studio musicians hired by Disney to accompany the actress.

2. How was the message produced and conveyed? The message of this text is many-layered. It is part of a larger television show—the audience (both in the studio and watching it on television) is assumed to know the greater context, that Hannah Montana is a fictional teenaged pop singer singing a song created by someone else. The audience is faceless, and the camera focuses entirely upon the main character of the media series, the teenaged girl singer. The audience is enthusiastic, however, and choreographed with their hands in the air, holding glowing sticks that they wave rhythmically in time to the music. The sound and lighting quality are top-notch, and the result is a slickly produced moment of television that is in keeping with a larger vision of the show.

3. How was the message organized, and what does it mean? This clip shares with the *Pancake Mountain* clip the same kind of organization, one self-contained song focusing upon a band in the commonly recognized genre of music video. The "plot" of the clip revolves around the rising action, climax, and falling action of the song itself, and the camera, lighting and sound all work to promote and further this musical "plot." The meaning of this clip to its participants is to enjoy watching one particular singer sing a song, not for a didactic purpose, but for the purpose of high-quality, highly-produced entertainment.

The second example is a music video clip from *Pancake Mountain* (found on YouTube: http://www.youtube.com/watch?v=DMGEt_k643Q), showcasing the band Kings of Leon, a garage-rock band with punk roots. The social-semiotic meaning of this clip of the same music video genre, contrasted with Hannah Montana, reveals a different message.

1. Who created the message? *Pancake Mountain* is the production company behind this clip. Compared to Disney, the corporate holdings are miniscule, and the production quality relatively poor. On stage, the message is created by many people, including the band (Kings of Leon), as well as the audience who was asked to participate in the production. The studio and production quality reflect the ethos of *Pancake Mountain*, that a greater didactic message of participation and enjoyment is more important than the quality of the production.

2. How was the message produced and conveyed? The creators of *Pancake Mountain* assume a certain amount of insider knowledge about the indie band scene. The audience is drawn from fans of Kings of Leon and their children, and the production relies upon word of mouth and website to create buzz for the show. The camera is hand-held, moving jaggedly through the shots, and the focus cuts from wide-angled shots of the band to close-ups on band members as well as the energetic, enthusiastic audience. The band plays with the audience instead of toward it, meaning that the audience has faces, reinforcing the ethos of participation in creative acts. Wardrobe and set design are amateur and (in the case of the audience) from the participants' own closets, which helps to create a sense of inclusion among television viewers as well. Unlike on *Hannah Montana*, a posh wardrobe isn't necessary to take part in this activity.

3. How was the message organized, and what does it mean? This music video also follows the flow of the musical text, emphasizing the song's frenetic energy through a focus upon action, both the band's actions and the audience's. At a few points the camera halts upon a boy who is dancing energetically to the music in a relatively clear space. The boy is not famous, like Hannah Montana or Kings of Leon, but the emphasis upon this relatively unknown person helps to promote the underlying DIY ethos that everyone can participate in making and enjoying music.

The unproduced qualities of *Pancake Mountain* are revealed by the focus of the message's organization and production. Unlike *Hannah Montana*, which emphasized a larger storyline about a fictional girl with exemplary qualities of an upper-middle-class pop star, the message of *Pancake Mountain*'s music video clip focused primarily upon an "unproduced" quality that allows the audience to feel included in, rather than set at a distance from, the text. We have identified two features of *Pancake Mountain* that make the children's television show pedagogically useful for exploring critical media literacy and convergence and for engaging youth in "unproduction": 1) The (DIY) Do-It-Yourself punk ethic; and, 2) Anticommercialism and anti-merchandising plotlines and musical guests. We develop these aspects below, using examples specifically taken from episodes #1 and #2 on the first DVD.

The DIY Approach

Pancake Mountain emerged from a do-it-yourself subculture that began during the punk movement. During the 1970s punk music surfaced as a working class alternative to the mainstream music industry, offering "something new and liberating through its independent and 'do-it-yourself' approach" (Triggs, 2006, p. 70). *Pancake Mountain* draws on such a DIY ethic that encourages individuals to "make your own culture and stop consuming that which is made for you" (Duncombe, 1997, p.1-2). Through its low-budget quality, *Pancake Mountain* offers a critique of commercially produced and packaged children's television programming. Appropriating discourses of mainstream media and popular culture is another means by which *Pancake Mountain* critiques commercially produced children's television. Skits such as the *Pancake Mountain News with Rock Rodgers* parody the evening news broadcast, where inane human-interest stories and product placements substitute for hard-hitting news stories about global and local events or politics. Consider this example from episode 2 where news anchor Rock Rodgers reports on the Annual *Groovy Juvy* Cola 4th of July parade:

> Rock Rodgers: The Annual Fourth of July *Groovy Juvy* Independence Day parade went off without a hitch despite heavy rains, dangerous flooding and angry badgers. Our fair city took a real soaking but spirits were not dampened. Good citizens crowded the parade route in rambunctious celebration and festive festivities. Police reported few fatalities, mostly involving poorly grounded electric flags and skirmishes over free goodies. For more on this annual celebration we are joined by our very own Joey Fiola. So Joey, how did this glorious celebration of independence go?
>
> Joey Fiola: (*standing under an umbrella in the pouring rain*) To tell you the truth, Rock, it was a lot of rain and not much fun.

In this news story segment, through the use of downplay and understatement the evening news is parodied. Such instances of downplay are noticeable in the lines: "despite heavy rains, dangerous flooding and angry badgers," "our fair city took a real soaking but spirits were not dampened," and "police reported few fatalities, mostly involving poorly grounded electric flags and skirmishes over free goodies." Downplay is coupled with Joey Fiola's understatement ("it was a lot of rain and not much fun"), highlighting how oftentimes on the evening news the negative is minimized in order to present stories in a naively positive manner.

Another feature of the show that undermines commercially produced television is Rufus Leaking's entertainment reporting, where Rufus, a goat sock puppet, interviews members of popular independent rock bands. Take this skit from episode 5, for instance, where Rufus interviews three members of the jam band Widespread Panic, Dave Schools, Todd Nance, and Sonny Ortiz.

> RL: You guys did a video with the Bad Santa guy, right?
> Todd: Yeah we did. Billy Bob Thornton.
> RL: Is he as scary as he seems?
> Todd: Ah, scarier.

RL: Yeah, I figured because I was thinking about having him direct me in a video, but the guy gives me the creeps, frankly.

RL: Now this next question is for Dave. Dave, you do a lot of side projects outside of the group. Do you ever say to yourself, "self, I'm too good for these guys? I'm outta here."

Dave: Oh yeah. All the time but they—

Todd: We keep telling him that too, but he doesn't listen to us. (laughing)

Dave: They have a lot of information on me that I don't want the rest of the world to know about. So, I'm pretty much in their hip pocket.

Todd: (laughing)

RL: So let me ask you guys this. Did you start out as a low level anxiety and maybe moved up to a localized panic? Or were you just Widespread Panic right from the start?

Todd: We rose to failure. That was our beginnings.

RL: I see.

Dave: We were just plain old "Panic."

RL: Just panic.

Dave: Just plain old "Panic."

RL: Then it started to spread a little bit.

Sonny: Then we became widespread.

Todd: Well ya know, the meals [patting stomach] got better ya know—

RL: Got it.

Todd: You understand that.

Dave: I thought this was a kids' show.

RL: It is a kids' show but it's also a medical show.

Sonny: Crossing that field...

Dave: Forensics?

RL: Yeah. That's right.

(laughing)

RL: Alright. This is my last question. And it's probably the most important, so please consider your answer carefully.

Dave: Okay.

RL: Stephanie Seymour or Erin Everly, who is better for Axl Rose?

Todd: Erin Everly.

Sonny: Erin. Erin.

RL: I agree completely. Good answer.

In interviewing Widespread Panic, Rufus Leaking parodies the question-posing practices of journalists who appear on entertainment news shows. In the interview above, such instances of parody are noticeable when Rufus Leaking asks the band members about making a music video with the actor Billy Bob Thornton from the motion picture Bad Santa (Coen, Coen & Zwigoff, 2003). Instead of asking what would be considered a more typical question, "what was that experience like?" Rufus Leaking poses the unexpected, "Is he as scary as he seems?" The sense of parody continues when Rufus Leaking inquires into the origins of the band's name, asking: "Did you start out as a low level anxiety and maybe moved up to a localized panic? Or were you just Widespread Panic right from the start?" And finally, the interview ends with Rufus Leaking posing an inane and unrelated question about Guns N' Roses' lead singer Axl Rose's former girlfriends: "Stephanie Seymour or Erin Everly, who is better for Axl Rose?" Such questions assume a certain kind of background knowledge, that the show's young viewers may or may not have access to, yet their parents might. Through segments such as these, *Pancake Mountain* offers a different expectation for the viewer, creating an experience that young children can only fully comprehend with the assistance of a parent or adult.

Under the "fanfare" section of the show's website, many newspaper and magazine articles can be accessed that outline the show's creation and how it engages with a DIY ethic. For example, a 2003 article in the *Washington City-Paper*, a free weekly newspaper, has this title: *Youth Brigade: The creators of Pancake Mountain hope to bring their old-school-punk aesthetic to the kid-vid set*. In this article, the author describes the show's connection to the punk movement:

> Although getting older, having kids, and recording music to appeal to one's progeny may not seem punk, Stuckey says that *Pancake Mountain* adheres to the genre's values. "It's still the do-it-yourself movement," he says. "The punk people involved don't necessarily sound punk, but what started the punk scene is driving us." (Godfrey, 2003, n.p.)

In engaging with the relationship between *Pancake Mountain* and the punk movement, educators can highlight how such a DIY ethic can enable youth to not only be "consumers" but also "producers "of popular culture. Using materials on hand, youth can engage in re-visioning mainstream media and popular culture. Some questions that students might be encouraged to ask about *Pancake Mountain's* background relate to extending the show's imaginative universe into their own creative work. Students can explore *Pancake Mountain's* genre, music shows geared toward their demographic, and discuss ways that this show uses the DIY ethic to unproduce, or strip down the normal trappings of commercial productions to create anti-consumer meanings. Students can extrapolate the DIY philosophy to their involvement with other media. Using *Pancake Mountain* as a guideline, what other kinds of shows can they unproduce so that new messages and meanings can emerge? Does a particular television show fairly portray all of the characters? How might the story be re-visioned and revised from the point of view of this character? Are there other stories that could be told in this universe? Poaching (de Certeau, 1984; Jenkins, 2006) these texts by rewriting them allows students to understand that stories and messages from the media are permeable and situational.

Another engagement that could follow discussing *Pancake Mountain's* punk roots might be to show a clip from the show and to explain the definition of convergence. Then, students could be asked to search the *Pancake Mountain* website for places of convergence. At what point does the show reveal interest in anti-consumer culture? *Pancake Mountain*'s website uses popular kinds of media message proliferation, but for what purpose? As the website's "consumer," what messages are students taking from the *Pancake Mountain* website as opposed to other websites that are also geared toward the students' demographic (such as the *Hannah Montana* website, http://tv.disney.go.com/disneychannel/hannahmontana/), and in what ways are these websites positioning them differently? How does the use of free means of online media distribution, such as YouTube, change the nature of the message that the media sends?

Anti-commercialism and Anti-merchandising Plotlines

The bulk of *Pancake Mountain*'s narrative energy is invested in critiquing forms of convergence, particularly the commercialism and merchandising associated with popular children's media. Steinberg and Kincheloe (2004) use the term "kinderculture" to refer to "the corporate children's consumer culture, [which] commodifies cultural objects and turns them into things to purchase rather than objects to contemplate" (p. 11). According to Steinberg and Kincheloe (2004):

> Kinderculture is produced by ingenious marketers who possess profound insights into the lives, desires, and cultural context of contemporary children. Such marketers know how to cultivate intense affect among children and use such emotion to elicit particular consumptive and in turn ideological reactions. (p. 11)

Because of its ability to construct childhood, youth and adults must together engage in a criticism of kinderculture. Such criticism can enable youth and adults to understand how commercial youth culture often positions children as passive consumers. Such criticism is especially salient in light of the fact that "in the late twentieth and early twenty-first centuries corporate-produced children's culture has replaced schooling as the producer of the central curriculum of childhood" (p. 11). In this way, critical inquiry into the effects of kinderculture on the lives and experiences of youth should be a main concern for literacy educators. We see *Pancake Mountain* as offering a text that literacy educators can draw on for supporting inquiry into the corporate production of child culture.

For example, in episode 1, Captain Perfect enters the manager's office and sees on his desk a plastic pancake frisbee with a note that reads "From the Desk of Neal: Possible merchandising—Neal." He takes the note and the frisbee to two other members of *Pancake Mountain*, JR and Caz, who are meeting together to discuss show ideas in the lounge. The following exchange takes place:

> CP: [bursts in lounge] Caz, JR, I've got to talk to you. This is important.
> Caz: Slow down, what is it?
> JR: Yeah did the kids give you another wedgie?
> CP: Even worse. Look at this! [hands them the plastic pancake Frisbee].
> Caz: What is it?
> CP: It's merchandising! Can't you see what the "board" is up to?
> Caz: [Holding pancake] You must be mistaken—
> JR: Again [laughing].
> CP: Come on guys. This is serious.
> Caz: Look. You know, we all agreed on this show that we would never sell this kind of cheap commercial product.
> JR: Especially something as ugly as this.
> Caz: And it's heavy! This could really hurt somebody [accidentally hitting JR in the face and knocking him off his chair].
> CP: Cheap merchandising! Cheap merchandising!
> Caz: Get a grip on yourself. This does not mean that it is possible merchandising.
> CP: Oh yeah, well look at this note I found [holding up note taken from Neal's desk].

This exchange between Captain Perfect, JR, and Caz highlights *Pancake Mountain's* commitment to not develop a line of merchandising to accompany the show. In fact, in the scene that follows, we learn that Captain Perfect believes the children of *Pancake Mountain* are too smart to fall for "cheap" merchandising. Sitting in the conference room with four board members, Captain Perfect protests the board's plans to sell "cheap merchandise to the children of *Pancake Mountain*":

> BM #1: One word for you [holds up Frisbee]... merchandising.
> BM #2: What is that?
> BM #1:This is a "Flapjack Flyer" [throws it across conference table and it hits Captain Perfect who falls out of his chair]. Tie it in to a toy company and we take this baby coast-to-coast.
> BM #2: You might have something. Gentleman, I think we have a plan. It's a go.
> CP: No!
> BM #1: Sorry Mr. Perfect. That's the way things are.
> CP: That's do-do. The kids in DC, they want quality. They don't want this cheap, cheesy stuff.
> BM #1: We prefer to think of it as cost effective. Besides this research shows...
> CP: Research? Research this ... [jumps on board table]
> BM #2: [on phone] Get me security.
> A security guard enters. After some struggle, Captain Perfect is carried out of the room.
> BM #2: I think, considering everything, that went quite well.

This scene is intended as a satire of U.S. business culture where board members make decisions based solely on the bottom line and are mostly European American males, wearing business suits. To highlight the satirical aspects of this scene one of the board members is dressed as a hipster, and the other is played by Bob Mould of the legendary punk band Hüsker Dü. Captain Perfect, an ally of children, is the foil to these businessmen, suggesting that any decision made with the bottom line as its concern cannot be in the best interest of children.

Some questions that students might be asked about this clip are, Who has the power in this clip? How is power questioned? How does the creator and writers of *Pancake Mountain* invite viewers to critique power? What power relations might the creator have had to negotiate in order to make this show available to others?

Another activity that could follow this engagement would be to poach (Jenkins, 1992) or appropriate the scene to make it their own. That is, students could revise the boardroom scene to reflect other social issues that they find important. Students could engage with this idea of poaching by perusing the school or city newspaper to identify a locally relevant issue. Then, students could revoice the satirical boardroom discussion using their identified issue. In the tradition of Boal (1985), students could perform an impromptu acting exercise that is related to social action. The humor of the boardroom scene would contribute to making immediately relevant issues accessible to students, and each side of the issue could shift to enable students to revoice the issue, allowing for multiple perspectives.

To unproduce the commercial aspects of childhood culture, teachers might also engage students in analyzing the musical guests that appear on *Pancake Mountain*. Most of the musicians and bands that perform on the show's "dance party" segment are from independent record labels. In the second episode, the reggae band Steel Pulse sings "we don't want no weapons of mass destruction." Throughout the show's 10 episodes, none of the musical guests are entertainers who specifically are marketed toward children. In considering who is invited to perform on *Pancake Mountain*, youth might be encouraged to question how viewers are positioned: What viewers might feel like "outsiders" when viewing the musical performances? How do musical performances position children as consumers of entertainment? How is the positioning similar to/different from the positioning in other forms of entertainment targeted at children?

Finally, the *Pancake Mountain News* segment offers another forum for critiquing "kinderculture." In episode 2, news anchorman Rock Rogers reports that the Groovy Juvy Cola Company has become the official sponsor of *Pancake Mountain*. Showing a clip of two European American men dressed in business suits, shaking hands as they pass each other in yellow taxi cabs, Rogers comments:

> WPB-TV CEO Mr. Bumper shown here with Groovy Juvy chairman Thurston Fister-tintin approved a three-year deal for an undisclosed amount. Groovy Juvy produces a full-line of top-rated, quality food-related products [*holding a can of* Groovy Juvy cola] for the whole family. Groovy Juvy cola, as you know, is a delightful, fruity, refreshing beverage, sure to keep you cool in summer and warm in winter [*takes a drink of the cola*]. Ah.

In response to this "fake" news story, students might be prompted to ask, "What real information might we learn from this 'fake' news story? How is this 'fake' story perhaps more real than the so-called 'real' stories that appear in the mainstream media? (Trier, 2008b, p. 604). Also following Trier's (2008b) recommendation, teachers might consider showing the "fake" news stories that regularly appear on *Pancake Mountain* alongside mainstream news stories. For instance, Trier (2008b) suggests that students consider how a news event or figure is treated on mainstream news as opposed to "fake" news shows, like the *Daily Show*.

This activity reflects upon one of the threads of our discussion, the importance of taking and teaching a critical stance in relation to the media, a stance that will enable students to question the glut of media messages that they encounter daily.

Conclusion

Unproducing can be an important tool in a culture that is becoming more oriented toward all-encompassing media from large media conglomerates. Although convergence culture offers media consumers many ways to enter into a dialogue with the larger company that sponsors the media, it is important to remember that grass-roots creativity can also change the way media works. *Pancake Mountain* is one of a few kinds of unproduced media that empowers children to envision and enact their own creative works. Other avenues for this creativity are self-published zines and blogs, original creative fiction published on the internet, and a host of creative endeavors that can now be supported by and stimulated by new technologies.

References

Alvermann, D., Moon, J.S., & Hagood, M.C. (1999). *Popular culture in the classroom: Teaching and researching critical media literacy.* Newark, DE: International Reading Association.

Black, R. W. (2008). *Adolescents and online fan fiction.* New York: Peter Lang.

Boal, A. (1985). *Theater of the oppressed.* New York: Theater Communications Group, Inc.

Coen J., & Coen E. (Producers), & Zwigoff, T. (Director). (2003). *Bad Santa* [Motion picture]. USA: Columbia Pictures.

Cyrus, M. (Performer) & Poryes, M. (Producer). (2006). *Hannah Montana* [Music video]. Retrieved Dec. 10, 2008 from http://www.youtube.com/watch?v=rBjyhVzCIhw

de Certeau, M. (1984). *The practice of everyday life.* Berkeley: UC Press.

Duncombe, S. (1997). *Notes from the underground: Zines and the politics of alternative culture.* Bloomington, IN: Verso.

Godfrey, S. (2003). Youth brigade: The creators of *Pancake Mountain* hope to bring their old-school-punk aesthetic to the kid-vid set. *Washington City Paper.* Retrieved March 16, 2009 from http://www.pancakemountain.com/articles/press_wcp.htm

Heim, J. (2005). On TV's "Pancake Mountain:" Hot bands playing with hip tots. *The Washington Post.* Retrieved March 16, 2009 from http://www.pancakemountain.com/articles/press_wpost.htm

Jenkins, H. (1992). *Textual poachers: Television fans and participatory culture.* New York: Routledge.

Jenkins, H. (2006). *Fans, bloggers, and gamers: Exploring participatory culture.* New York: NYU Press.

Kings of Leon (Songwriter & Performer) & Stuckey, S. (Videoproducer). (2008). *Kings of Leon / Pancake Mountain* [Music video]. Retrieved Dec. 10, 2008 from http:// www.youtube.com/watch?v=DMGEt_k643Q

Kress, G. (2003). *Literacy in the new media age.* New York: Routledge.

O'Sullivan, M. (2006). Nothing syrupy about "Pancake." *The Washington Post.* Retrieved March 16, 2009 from http://www.pancakemountain.com/articles/press_wp.htm

Steinberg, S. & Kincheloe, J. (Eds.). (2004). *Kinderculture: The corporate construction of childhood* (2nd ed.). Boulder, CO: Westview Press.

Stone, J. C. (2007). Popular websites in adolescents' out-of-school lives: Critical lessons on literacy. In M. Knobel, & C. Lankshear, (Eds.), *A new literacies sampler* (pp. 49-65). New York: Peter Lang.

Thomas, A. (2007). *Youth online: Identity and literacy in the digital age.* New York: Peter Lang.

Trier, J. (2008a). *The Daily Show with Jon Stewart*: Part 1. *Journal of Adolescent & Adult Literacy, 51*(5), 424-427.

Trier, J. (2008b). *The Daily Show with Jon Stewart*: Part 2. *Journal of Adolescent & Adult Literacy, 51*(7), 600-605.

Triggs, T. (2006). Scissors and glue: Punk fanzines and the creation of a DIY aesthetic. *Journal of Design History (19)*1, 69-83.

Tucker, C. (2007). *Pancake Mountain–Preschool of punk and DIY*. Retrieved March 23, 2009 from http://www.pancakemountain.com/articles/press_anthem.htm

CHAPTER THREE

Adolescents' Explorations with Do-It-Yourself Media
Authoring Identity in Out-of-School Settings

BARBARA J. GUZZETTI

Of all the new literacy practices that adolescents engage in today, perhaps the most empowering are those of participatory or do-it-yourself (DIY) media. These are forms of literate practice that young people engage with outside of school in creating their own alternative texts. These DIY media are empowering in that they allow youth to express themselves and fill a void, such as serving as a vehicle for writing on topics that are typically not taken up in institutional settings of schools or addressed by the commercial press in teen magazines. These new media allow young people more freedom of expression and autonomy than they experience inside of classrooms (Ito et al., 2008).

DIY media have expanded not only in their content and form but also in the contexts in which they are produced. Today's youth use and produce virtually every medium, including film, music, periodicals, and websites to express themselves, to form and represent their identities, and to connect with others (Kearney, 2006). Their DIY media encompass print, digital, hybrid, and lyrical texts that have shifted from being produced only in clandestine settings of adolescents' bedrooms to being created, broadcast, and archived worldwide through the internet. For example, zines (self-published alternatives to commercial magazines) are now being produced and shared across the globe on the internet as e-zines; indie (independent) music is self-recorded on CDs or archived on indie music websites; and independent films are appearing in international film festivals or in YouTube videos on the web.

My purpose in taking up the topic of DIY media is to raise educators' awareness of the wide range of form and content of these alternative texts and to describe the appealing elements of these new literacies. In doing so, I hope to be able to identify those features of DIY media that will be useful to teachers and other adults who interact with young people in connecting with and understanding adolescents' interests and alternative forms of literate expression. By learning about the existence of these DIY media, teachers may see their students who produce them in new ways and recognize young people for their literate accomplishments in other settings.

Adolescents' production of DIY media addresses the concern expressed about young people's seeming engagement in merely passive consumption of corporate owned and profit-driven content that has been identified by other researchers (Black & Steinkuehler, 2009; Steinkuehler, 2007). By learning the reasons that adolescents create these texts, the voids that they fill, and the opportunities they provide in adolescents' literate lives, teachers may become aware of new ways to motivate their students. In describing these new literacies, I hope to enable educators to recognize the appealing features of these new literate practices that may be transferable to instruction.

Like my colleagues who have written on new digital literacies (Black & Steinkuehler, 2009), I caution that this chapter deals with those adolescents who have the resources (e.g., time, access, and in some cases, finances) to create these alternative texts. Not all students have equal opportunities to engage in DIY media practices due to various contextual conditions, such as demands of part-time jobs, low socioeconomic status, or a lack of peer support. Hence, there may be students who have not heard of let alone produced or consumed these do-it-yourself media. Therefore, raising teachers' awareness of these media may also result in raising students' understandings as teachers become more cognizant and appreciative of their students' informal literacies.

In taking up the topic of DIY media, I also wish to alert educators that simply co-opting these practices for classroom instruction may be inappropriate depending on the nature of these practices. In some studies, the students who create DIY media such as zines have cautioned that making them classroom assignments would destroy the pleasure that they get from creating these texts and would quash the subversive nature of these new literacies (Guzzetti & Gamboa, 2004a; Knobel & Lankshear, 2001). Hence, one of my goals in this chapter is to inform educators about the intriguing elements of these practices that may be transferable to and appropriate for creating literacy activities in classroom settings that appeal to today's millennial youth. Another of my goals is to demonstrate that the new literate practices inherently require creative and literate expression, thereby allowing teachers a new perspective on students who may otherwise go unnoticed or be marginalized in classroom settings.

Toward these goals, I first define and explain the key constructs that this chapter addresses as an orientation to the concepts in the chapter. These new conceptual terms include the term "DIY media" that I use to refer to participatory media, and my rationale for choosing this term as a rubric for these new literacy practices. I also provide my working definition of an adolescent and describe the nature of adolescence in the new times of the new millennium. Finally, I discuss the notion of new literacies.

In the second part of this chapter, I review the extant research on adolescents' creations of the lesser-known forms of DIY media, and the offline places and online spaces where they are shared and promoted. These DIY media include user-created video games; digital films, such as machinima and stop-motion videos created in offline places and online spaces of virtual worlds; zines and e-zines, and the Distros and infoshops (distribution centers) where they are often found; and indie music shared through fans' cybersites. My discussion of these media texts also includes a depiction of the fans who create, facilitate, distribute, and promote these self-created media.

In the final section of this chapter, I synthesize the common appealing features of these forms of DIY media. Some of these features have been identified by researchers who explored these media themselves while others have been described by the young people who create them. In conclusion, I offer implications for teaching and learning with DIY media in content classrooms, including those suggested by the adolescents who have produced these new literacies.

Orientation

DIY Media

Do-it-yourself (DIY) media have also been referred to as new media, alternative media, participatory media, and indie media. Although each of these terms is not quite an accurate rubric, in this chapter I use the term "DIY media" to refer to those literacies that put young people at the forefront in creating their own texts. The notion of DIY media implies the element of self-creation that characterizes these literate practices.

I also choose the term DIY media partly because other terms are misnomers. For example, the term "new media" is actually inaccurate because some of the new media practices that constitute the new literacies (which have only recently been recognized by educators) actually have a long history. Zines are one example as they began appearing in the 1930s as fanzines created by fans of *Superman* and other adventure comics that now have evolved to personal, political or themed zines. The term "indie media" has been most closely associated with independent newspapers and periodicals and therefore does not capture the range of literacy practices that adolescents create by themselves and for themselves. The term "participatory media" implies a more passive role than that which adolescents take up in creating these media. This term also does not capture the notion that adolescents often create DIY media on their own without assistance from others. Finally, the term "alternative media" is too vague to characterize these practices and sets up a false dichotomy between in-school academic literacies and DIY out-of-school literacies

Even the term "DIY media" is not the perfect rubric, however. This term can be misleading because many of the do-it-yourself literacies that adolescents create may be facilitated by commercial products, such as video games that allow players the capacity for "modding" or creating their own video games as extensions of popular computer games. Yet, the term do-it-yourself (DIY) media best captures the spirit with which adolescents enter into these new literate practices and the ways in which they create these texts. Therefore, it is with the caveat of the possibility of an association with commercial products that I choose to use the term "DIY media" in this chapter to refer to adolescents' self-created media.

Today's Adolescent and the Nature of Adolescence

In examining the DIY media that young people create in out-of-school settings, it is both necessary and useful to examine the term "adolescent" in light of these media and to characterize the nature of adolescence in these new times. Most of the research on DIY media that I review in this chapter has focused on how young people ages 12-21 produce and consume these texts. Some researchers have used the term adolescent to refer to this more inclusive age range and think of adolescence more in social terms than in terms of chronological age (e.g., Alvermann, 2007).

Some researchers, such as Alvermann (2009) and Black and Steinkuehler (2009) have troubled the term "adolescent." Black and Steinkuehler consider "adolescent" to be a nebulous term, but settle on defining adolescence as a transition period between childhood and adulthood (Lesko, 2001). This definition characterizes an adolescent as a cultural construction. Other researchers, such as Alvermann (2009) eschew the view of an adolescent as a person who is less than an adult. Rather, a new trend is to focus on young people's competencies as facile users and creators of new technologies and media forms, by viewing an adolescent as someone who is merely different than an adult. Recently, researchers have noted that effective educators view adolescents not from a deficit view or as individuals in crisis, but as those who have agency, whose expertise can be used and fostered in classrooms (e.g., Alvermann, 2009; Christenbury, Bomer & Smagorinsky, 2009). This perspective characterizes adolescents from a sociocultural viewpoint and speaks to the empowering nature of new media practices that put young people at the forefront in taking leadership in creating new textual forms. This theory recognizes adolescence as a period of extensive social and cognitive growth (Langer, 2009).

These new views of adolescents and adolescence require a shift in the way that teachers view their students and how they design and implement instruction. By recognizing that young people can be leaders in establishing and creating new forms of media, teachers may find it motivating and informative to provide students with opportunities to discuss and/or display their DIY media in classroom settings. In these cases, young people may provide their teachers and peers with lessons on the benefits of engaging in these new literacies by describing the social and technological skills they acquire in creating media that enable them to participate in contemporary society. Later in this chapter, I will return to this idea and describe how teachers may appropriately structure peer-based learning in exploring the new literacies of DIY media.

New Literacies

Leu (2002) defined the new literacies as "the skills, strategies and insights necessary to successfully exploit the rapidly changing information and communication technologies that continuously emerge in our world" (p. 313). The New London Group (1996) described literacies as those that entail sense making within a rich multimodal semiotic system situated in a community of practice. Other researchers identified new literacies as those literate practices that are either digital or post-typographic or those that are relatively new in chronological terms or are new to being thought of as literacy practices (Lankshear & Knobel, 2003). Examples of new digital literacies include navigating and constructing web sites (Guzzetti, 2007), participating in electronic message boards and e-discussion lists (Guzzetti, 2008b); blogging (Davies & Merchant, 2007), and online journaling (Guzzetti & Gamboa, 2005). Examples of new literacies that are print based and have only recently been recognized as literate practices include zining (Knobel & Lankshear, 2001) and creating lyrical texts of independent (indie) music, such as video game music and punk rock (Guzzetti & Yang, 2005).

As Lankshear and Knobel (2003) note, some of these new literacy practices may be sustained over time while others may quickly come and go. In addition, as new technology advances other digital literacy practices may appear. For example, in some Asian countries moblogging (sending text messages from a cell phone to a weblog) is a common digital literacy practice that may become more popular in the United States as more people take up the practice of blogging and use cell phones instead of or in addition to land lines. Hence, the term new literacies may be difficult to define due to the changing nature of emerging technologies (Leu, 2006).

Adolescents' Engagement in DIY Media

This section of the chapter describes the most popular new literacy practices that represent DIY media and those that researchers have taken up in their investigations of adolescents' participation in new literacies. These include young peoples' engagement in digital literacies, such as modding or creating video games from commercial games, participating, creating, and constructing texts in virtual worlds, e-zining (writing zines online), blogging, and online journaling. These DIY media also include print-based literacies, such as producing and consuming zines and creating the lyrical texts of independent music and participating in their associated web sites, message boards, and electronic discussion lists. In reviewing the research on adolescents' participation in these DIY media practices, I also address how these do-it-yourself media are facilitated by new structures and platforms that support and encourage their creation.

Constructing Video Games

The new literacies of video games have been described by other researchers (e.g., Gee, 2003; Steinkuehler, 2007). This new literacy practice includes both traditional and new forms of literate practices required by gaming, such as discerning overlapping conversations and activities, reading and writing texts to other players, and the production and consumption of orally delivered narratives and poetry (Steinkuehler, 2007). Hence, educational researchers have considered video gaming as an activity that does not replace literacy activities but is an actual literate activity, albeit a new one (Gee, 2003; Steinkuehler, 2007).

The term "modding" is a slang expression that means modifying. In relation to video games, the term refers to the act of modifying software to perform a function not originally conceived by the designer. Modding is often referred to within the Open Source software movement and within the computer game community and implies creating new or altered video-game content and sharing that content through the internet.

Some video game companies actively encourage modding or hacking in which video gamers change parts or all of a game by altering its code by supplying the tools to do so (Hyman, 2004). Unlike the music and film industries that protect their property and discourage fans from altering or copying their content, some video-game manufacturers have been changing outdated notions of copyright by providing these tools (Gee, 2007). One popular video game is *Counter-Strike*, which is based on a mod of the game *Half-Life*. Since mods cannot be created without first owning an original retail version, it has quickly become apparent that mods have a positive effect on the sale of the video games on which they are based (Hyman, 2004). Manufacturers have discovered that modding extends the shelf life of video games and helps to build community (Hyman, 2004). These communities often take the form of groups of players who work together over the internet and never see each other face-to-face yet create new video games by using free software from the game companies to create video games that are "as good or better than the original commercially available games" (Gee, 2003, p. 195). Modders may change the difficulty level of the game, the style of play, and the ability to solve problems in varying and multiple ways. For example, games like *Civilization* have built-in modding tools that allow players to create new "maps" of the world. Other video games provide modding tools that allow players to modify content ranging from quests to avatar appearance.

According to Gee (2003), good video games allow players to be more than passive consumers. They are also active producers who can customize their own learning experiences. Modding allows students to be insiders in creating their own knowledge and skills. Gee notes that this ability is in sharp contrast to adolescents' typical experiences in classrooms where they are often simply passive consumers and where the teacher is the insider and the learner is an outsider.

My own research with adolescents on their out-of-school interactions with forensics-related video games (Guzzetti, 2008a) identified the intriguing elements of these computer games for young people. The adolescents I spoke with and played commercial video games with enjoyed the opportunity to use their observation and inference skills that they learned in science classes to predict, piece clues together, and think ahead in solving crimes, such as those presented in the video games *Murder on the Orient Express, CSI: Three Dimensions of Murder,* and the Nancy Drew video games of *Stayed Tuned for Danger* and *Secrets Can Kill*. These young people valued the interactivity and the sophisticated graphics in these mystery video games. Adolescent girls appreciated video games with female protagonists, such as the one found in the Agatha Christie video game, *Murder on the Orient Express* who actively pose questions and help solve crimes. In doing so, the game developers eschewed typical representations found in video games that have predominately male characters and represent females negatively as victims or objectify them as prizes (Provenzo, 1991).

Video games stimulate adolescents by putting them at the forefront in their own learning. Modding new video games from original ones can facilitate teenagers' ability to take center stage in learning by allowing them to create their own learning experiences and environments. Modding enables adolescents to develop games that challenge them.

To assess how well adolescents perform in science/technology, Gee (2003) posed the following questions: "How well can students leverage knowledge in others and in various tools and technologies? How are they positioned within a network that connects them in rich ways to other people and various tools and technologies?" (p. 189).

Modding addresses these skills and abilities through the attraction and power of collaborative knowledge production, an appealing element of video games (Gee, 2003; Leland, Harste & Kuonen, 2008). Young people have expressed their desires for opportunities to work interactively and collaboratively (Guzzetti, 2008); creating the digital texts of video games encourages and facilitates this type of learning environment. Adolescents are enabled to work together and form affinity groups (Gee, 2003), communities of practice, or fan groups that create and discuss this new literate practice. Video gamers advance community in their collaborative efforts in modding, their online meetings on web sites and their offline meetings in person at video game conventions, such as the MAGFest, the Mid-Atlantic Gaming Festival, an annual convention that celebrates video games and the culture they create.

Making DIY Films

It should also be noted that video games are the basis for other types of modding as well although these forms are just beginning to be explored by literacy researchers (e.g., Lankshear & Knobel, 2007; McClay, Mackey, Carbonaro, Szafron & Schaeffer, 2007). One of these forms is machinima. Machinima is a term derived from the combination of the words machine and cinema and refers to film production techniques that rely on computer-game software and engines from first-person shooter and role-playing simulation video games. Adolescents use traditional film-making techniques in a virtual environment to create their own movies from video game software. Examples of machinima can be found on Machinima.com, and the book *Machinima for Dummies* (Hancock & Ingram, 2007) provides directions for those with little or no prior experience in creating these DIY films.

Another DIY film-making technique is stop-motion animation, a technique that makes a physically manipulated object appear to move on its own. Young people create stop-action videos by photographing a series of small movements with digital cameras, uploading the photographs into the computer, and using video-editing software, such as Apple's iMovie. Adolescents can easily create stop-motion videos by getting directions from each other on the internet at sites such as StopMotionAnimation.com or on YouTube (www.YouTube.com) videos and can share their films through the internet.

Creating DIY Media in Virtual Worlds

Less attention has been paid in the literature to adolescents' participation in virtual worlds than to their other explorations in cyberspace. Virtual worlds (sometimes referred to as metaverses) are computer-based simulated environments intended for users (sometimes referred to as "residents") to inhabit and interact through motional characters called avatars. Perhaps the most popular of these is *Second Life (SL)*, a virtual world created almost entirely by its residents, and its counterpart, *Teen Second Life (TSL)*, designed for young people ages 13-17.

In *Second Life* and *Teen Second Life*, participants communicate through instant messaging, text chatting, and voice communications as they navigate, consume, and construct in this virtual world. Residents travel, explore, socialize, create, and trade virtual property and services. Although there are premium memberships that allow residents to build and sell property, a basic membership is free of charge, and there are many free goods and services residents provide to each other in *SL*.

Adolescents' interactions in virtual worlds, such as *The SIMS* and *Teen Second Life* have only recently become an area of inquiry for educational researchers and literacy scholars (e.g., Black & Steinkuehler, 2009; Boellerstorff, 2008; Thomas, 2007). Several new projects have begun that attempt to introduce adolescent girls to these virtual worlds, teach them digital literacies within the environments in which they are to be used, and research how participants learn to communicate, navigate, and produce digital structures and texts in virtual environments. Two examples of these girl-serving projects are *Tech Savvy Girls* (Hayes, Johnson, King, & Lammers, 2008), a project based both in *The Sims* and *Teen Second Life*, and *COMPUGIRLS* (Scott et al., 2008), a project in *TSL* that focuses on teaching girls of color who are underrepresented in technology fields the digital literacies to enable them to conduct community projects focusing on issues of social justice and write about and present their storied experiences to various audiences.

Teens who participated in other virtual world projects, such as the Schome National Association for Gifted and Talented Youth (NAGY) *Teen Second Life Project* and *Global Kids* (www.globalkids.org), a project based in New York City high schools designed to address social issues, developed a wide range of *Second Life* skills. These abilities included teleporting, building, scripting, and making videos and machinima in the virtual world that have real-world relevance. In addition to developing these digital literacies, participants enhanced their skills in communication, teamwork, leadership, and creativity (Open University Team, 2007).

The environment of *Teen Second Life* can facilitate not only the creation of new virtual and physical structures but also the production of new media texts. For example, a plethora of machinima produced by teens within *Second Life* can be found on YouTube (www.YouTube.com) videos. These include social justice projects, as *Global Kids Race to Equality: A Second Life Machinima* (http://www.YouTube/watch?v=HWT72e), in which teens are enabled through their avatars and *TSL* surroundings to story their first-life experiences of facing racial prejudice while growing up as children of color.

Adolescents who have not participated in these projects in virtual worlds have reported that they would be more interested, comfortable, and perform better in a class taught within virtual worlds due to the emphasis on cooperation rather than competition (Alverez, 2006). Learning the digital literacies required for today's technology through virtual worlds may appeal to adolescents due to the interactivity, communication, simulation, and navigation elements of these metaverses (Turkle, 1995). Youth may appreciate the capabilities of virtual worlds for forming and representing their identities through new digital forms and forums.

Virtual worlds also offer the unique benefits of situated and authentic learning. A virtual world such as *SL* or *TSL* can offer participants opportunities to gain situated understandings of digital literacies. For example, rather than learning abstractly about scripting languages for expressing programmed actions SL participants learn that some SL objects have associated actions that are added to the objects in the form of commands written in a particular way (see http://wiki.secondlife.com/wiki/LSL/Portal). This knowledge is embodied as "know how" in contrast to the "know what" that comprises more abstract understanding of concepts (Denning, 2004). This know how is reflected in the ability to engage in practices such as scripting while emphasizing the building blocks of such practices—the particular ways of thinking and acting that evolve from experience with tools and communities. *TSL* offers opportunities for learners to choose their own learning trajectories, gain social recognition, use multiple and integrated digital tools, and pursue numerous avenues of participation in communities of peers.

Authoring Zines and E-Zines

Zines (pronounced "Zeens") are self-created and self-published alternatives to commercial magazines authored and edited by young people; those who create them are called zinesters. Zines may take the form of personal zines (authoring one's own experiences with poetry and prose), themed zines (e.g., commercial fishing, skateboarding, thrift shopping) or political zines (e.g., feminist zines). They are based on the DIY ethic in that they fill a void in adolescents' lives by allowing them a space to express their ideas and voices on topics of personal interest to them that are often not sanctioned by the school or written about in commercial magazines aimed at young people (Guzzetti & Gamboa, 2004a).

Often, young people take up topics of social and gender justice in their zines. Adolescents write zines to question gendered representations of masculinity and femininity and question prejudiced views of racism, sexism and classism (Guzzetti & Gamboa, 2004a; 2004b). Youth write about various social problems, such as rape, self-injurious behavior, homophobia, and anorexia.

The format of zines, their shape, and their sizes are varied. Young people write their texts by using print, internet, and hybrid textual forms. Narratives, poetry, and prose are presented in ways that are characterized by pastiche and collage with backdrops and borders of graphics, photographs, illustrations, and words that complement and extend the pieces (Knobel & Lankshear, 2001). Although zines like other DIY media have been fostered by the advent of new technologies such as photocopies and computers (Jenkins, 2006) zinesters typically distribute their zines in hard copy at bookstores, alternative record stores, shows (concerts), and infoshops (political and feminist storehouses of information) so that those who do not have internet access can still read them. Other zinesters create e-zines by sharing them on the web though web sites or Distros (online distribution centers). They are distributed free of charge or for a nominal fee to cover the costs of copying and postage.

Zines have unique appeal for adolescents. Zines allow young people a freedom of expression in both choice of format and topic that they do not find in school (Knobel & Lankshear, 2001). Their zines are often written by using the expletives that characterize adolescents' talk and are written for and by each other. Zining appeals to adolescents' need for autonomy and independence as zines both foster and symbolize breaking free from oppressive rules and norms in both writing style and content.

Making Indie Music

Any discussion of DIY media would be remiss if it did not include independent or (indie) music. The DIY ethic has its roots in punk rock, a genre of indie music created by adolescents who were dissatisfied with commercial music. Punk rock started with adolescents creating alternative music in a garage and grew to become a music genre with subgenres, such as political punk, feminist punk, oi!, and street punk and an entire cultural movement with its own DIY ethic, style of dress, and dark imagery. Punk rock is characterized by repulsive band names (e.g., the Anal Cunt) and song titles (e.g., "I Got an Office Job for the Sole Purpose of Sexually Harassing Women") that are purposively intended to offend and insulate the subculture (Guzzetti & Yang, 2005).

Another genre of indie music is video game music. Adolescents who are members of bands like the Minibosses take the melodies or sounds from video games and transpose them into musical notes by using guitar for creating the high notes and the bass for the low notes, and adding in drum beats. Bands like the Minibossses are known for their video game music covers (musical pieces first performed and popularized by another artist), which are instrumental rock variations of the themes from classic Nintendo video games, such as Metroid, Mega Man, and Castlevania.

Video game music is played at video game conventions, and its fans visit the Minibosses' message board and indie music websites, such as VGMIx2.5.com (www.vgMix.com/vg25) to share, recognize, and celebrate this DIY music genre. A Dwelling of the Duels contest is conducted on this site to determine the best video game cover presented in the forum. The main function of this site is to promote and compete for awards for indie music.

Fans visit indie music cybersites to learn where and when bands like the Minibosses' shows will be held, as well as to network and communicate with each other. Hence, these cybersites have important functions for their members in enacting their identities as indie music fans both on and offline (Guzzetti, 2006; 2008b). The production of this music and the cybersites that support and promote these music genres assist fans to form a collaborative community by facilitating interactive production and consumption of these media.

Teaching and Learning with DIY Media

Looking across these DIY media, it can be readily noted that these new literacies have certain common elements. Each of these practices requires and promotes creativity, autonomy, and community. Most often, these DIY media are produced in atmospheres characterized by collaboration and interaction. As such, these new literacies represent and demonstrate the social nature of literacy (Street, 1995; Gee, 1996). These everyday literacies or vernacular literacies must be acknowledged and addressed in classrooms along with traditional academic literacy (Alvermann, 2007).

New environments such as virtual worlds are no better than face-to-face classrooms if learning and teaching are conceived in ways that simply mimic traditional education. New literacies researchers (Lankshear & Knobel, 2003) have described how the new digital literacies have been implemented in classrooms in ways that simply constitute "old wine in new bottles," such as using computers for word processing in writing essays or to keep track of students' grades. Teachers' reluctance to incorporate the multiliteracies associated with information and communication technologies may be due to a deficit view that engagement in noncanonical practices such as surfing the web or playing video games is not actual reading (Luke, 2001). Hence, incorporating the new literacies into classroom instruction may require a shift in the way that teachers define literacy and envision and implement literacy instruction.

The work of scholars and educators associated with the New Literacy Studies (e.g., Gee, 2006) has much to offer efforts to reconceptualize literacy education. From this perspective, computer-related learning is not mastery of isolated skills but learning to participate in new social practices and acquire new identities. Preparing youth to participate in living and working in the rapidly changing technological environment of the 21st century requires fostering adolescents' abilities to locate and solve problems, engage in complex situations and convert those situations into problems that can be solved, and learn how to learn (Bruce, 2001). Learners must be engaged in authentic tasks within communities where teachers serve as mentors who scaffold learning, engage learners in critical reflection, and support transfer of new practices to other contexts (New London Group, 1996).

One way to promote this type of learning environment is to allow young people to model and discuss their DIY media production and their products with other students. Youth respect one another's expertise and authority, particularly with digital literacies and are often more motivated to learn from peers than from adults (Ito et al., 2008). Although co-opting some DIY media such as zines as assignments is inappropriate, allowing adolescents to discuss their DIY creations can raise awareness of the literacy processes and practices that are often unrecognized and allow entrée into the Discourse community of literacy insiders (Gee, 1996).

Such activities can have several functions, the first of which is to demonstrate and facilitate the notion that it is not just schooling that teaches young people appropriate literacy practices. Teachers can build on the social nature of adolescents and promote the DIY ethic by designing collaborative and interactive literacy experiences that foster creativity and reward interactivity and collaboration. Rather than co-opting DIY media as school assignments and prostituting their nature, teachers can more appropriately foster the DIY ethos they represent. By acknowledging adolescents' literate abilities and accomplishments in out-of-school settings and by providing an atmosphere for instruction that fosters agency, teachers can successfully build on these DIY media.

References

Alverez, M. (2006). *Second Life and school: The use of virtual worlds in high school education.* Unpublished manuscript, San Antonio, Texas: Trinity University. Retrieved October 20, 2008 from http://ww.trinity.edu/adelwich/worlds/students.html

Alvermann, D.E. (2007). Redefining adolescent literacy instruction. In B. J. Guzzetti (Ed.), *Literacy for the new millennium: Adolescent literacy,* (pp. 3-10). Westport, CT: Praeger.

Alvermann, D.E. (2009). Sociocultural constructions of adolescence and young people's literacies. In L. Christenbury, R. Bomer, & P. Smagorinsky (Eds.) *Handbook of adolescent literacy research* (pp. 14-28). New York: Guilford.

Black, R.W., & Steinkuehler, C. (2009). Literacy in virtual worlds. In L. Christenbury, R. Bomer, & P. Smagorinsky (Eds.), *Handbook of adolescent literacy research* (pp. 271-287). New York: Guilford.

Boellerstorff, T. (2008). *Coming of age in Second Life: An anthropologist explores the virtually human.* Princeton, New Jersey: Princeton University Press.

Bruce, B. C. (2001). Diversity and critical social engagement: How changing technologies enable new modes of literacy in changing circumstances. In D. E. Alvermann (Ed.), *Adolescents and literacies in a digital world* (pp. 1-18). New York: Peter Lang.

Christenbury, L.L., Bomer, R., & Smagorinsky, P. (2009). *Handbook of adolescent literacy research.* New York: Guilford.

Davies, J., & Merchant, G. (2007). Looking from the inside out: Academic blogging as new literacies. In C. Lankshear & M. Knobel (Eds.), *New literacies sampler* (pp. 167-197). New York: Peter Lang.

Denning, P.J. (2004). The field of programmers myth. *Communications of the ACM, 47(7),* 15-20.

Gee, J.P. (1996). *Social linguistics and literacies* (2nd ed.). New York: Routledge Falmer.

Gee, J.P. (2003). *What video games have to teach us about literacy and learning.* New York: Palgrave Macmillan.

Gee, J.P. (2006). Why game studies now? Video games: A new art form. *Games and Culture, 1(1),* 58-61.

Gee, J.P. (2007). *What video games have to teach us about literacy and learning* (2nd ed.). New York: Palgrave Macmillan.

Guzzetti, B.J. (2006). Cybergirls: Negotiating identity on cybersites. *E-Learning, 3(2),* 158-169.

Guzzetti, B.J. (2008a, December). Adolescents' connections between everyday texts and their science learning in and out-of-school. In H. Harper (Chair),

Linking popular culture and internet texts to content instruction. Symposium conducted at the meeting of the National Reading Conference, Orlando, FL.

Guzzetti, B.J. (2008b). Identities in online communities: A young woman's critique of cyberculture. *E-Learning, 5*(4), 457-474.

Guzzetti, B.J. (2009). Lessons on literacy learning and teaching: Listening to adolescent girls. In L.L. Christenbury, R. Bomber, & P. Smagorinsky (Eds.), *Handbook of adolescent literacy research* (pp. 372-385). New York: Guilford.

Guzzetti, B.J. & Gamboa, M. (2004a). Zines for social justice: Adolescent girls writing on their own. *Reading Research Quarterly, 39* (4), 408-435.

Guzzetti, B.J., & Gamboa, M. (2004b). Zining: The unsanctioned literacy practice of adolescents. In C. Fairbanks, J. Worthy, B. Maloch, J. Hoffman, & D.L. Schallert (Eds.), *53rd Yearbook of the National Reading Conference,* (pp. 206-217). Oak Creek, WI: The National Reading Conference.

Guzzetti, B.J., & Gamboa, M. (2005). Online journaling: The informal writings of two adolescent girls. *Research in the Teaching of English, 40*(2), 168-206.

Guzzetti, B.J., & Yang, Y. (2005). Adolescents' punk rock fandom: Construction and production of lyrical texts. In B. Maloch, J.V. Hoffman. D.L. Schallert, C.M. Fairbanks, & J. Worthy (Eds.), *54th Yearbook of the National Reading Conference* (pp. 198-210), Oak Creek, WI: The National Reading Conference.

Hancock, H. & Ingram, J. (2007). *Machinima for dummies.* Hoboken, NJ: Wiley Publishing.

Hayes, E., Johnson, B., King, E., & Lammers, J. (2008, July). *The SIMS 2 and Teen Second Life: Insights from Year Two.* Paper presented at the meeting of the Games, Learning and Society Conference, Madison, WI.

Hyman, P. (2004). Video game companies encourage "modders." Retrieved November 14, 2008 from http://ww/hollywoodreporter.com/hr/search/article_display.jsp?vn

Ito, M., Horst, H., Bittanti, M., Boyd, D., Herr-Stephenson, B., Langs, P.E., Pascoe, C.J., Robinson, L. & Others (2008, November). *Living and learning with new media: Summary of findings from the Digital Youth Project.* Available: http://digitalyouth.inschool.berkeley.edu/files/report/digitalyouth-White Paper.pdf

Jenkins, H. (2006). *Fans, bloggers and gamers: Exploring participatory culture.* New York: New York University Press.

Kearney, M.C. (2006). *Girls make media.* New York: Routledge

Knobel, M., & Lankshear, C. (2001). Cut, paste, publish: The production and consumption of zines. In D.E. Alvermann (Ed.), *Adolescents and literacies in a digital world* (pp. 164-185). New York: Peter Lang.

Langer, J.A. (2009). Contexts for adolescent literacy. In L. Christenbury, R., Bomer, & P. Smagorinsky (Eds.), *Handbook of adolescent literacy research* (pp. 49-64). New York: Guilford.

Lankshear, C., & Knobel, M. (2003). *New literacies: Changing knowledge and classroom learning.* Buckingham, England: Open University Press.

Lankshear, C., & Knobel, M. (2007). Researching new literacies: Web 2.0 practices and insider perspectives. *E-Learning, 4*(3), 224-239.

Leland, C.H., Harste, J.C., & Kuonen, K. (2008). Unpacking videogames: Understanding and supporting a new ethos. In Y. Kim, V.J. Risko, D.L. Compton, D.K. Dickson, M.K. Hundley, R.T. Jimenez, K.M. Leader, & D.W. Rowe (Eds.), *57th Yearbook of the National Reading Conference* (pp. 231-340). Oak Creek, WI: The National Reading Conference.

Lesko, N. (2001). *Act your age: Cultural constructions of adolescence.* New York: Falmer.

Leu, D. (2002). The new literacies: Research on reading instruction with the internet. In A.E. Farstrup & S.J. Samuels (Eds.), *What research has to say about reading instruction (3rd ed.).* (pp. 310-316). Newark, DE: International Reading Association.

Leu, D. (2006). New literacies, reading research and the challenges of change: A deictic perspective. In J. Hoffman, D.L. Schallert, C.M. Fairbanks, J. Worthy & B. Maloch (Eds.), *55th Yearbook of the National Reading Conference* (pp. 1-20). Oak Creek, WI: National Reading Conference.

Luke, A. (2001). What happens to literacies old and new when they're turned into policy. In D.E. Alvermann (Ed), *Adolescents and literacies in a digital world* (pp. 132-146). New York: Peter Lang.

McClay, J.K., Mackey, M., Carbonaro, M., Szafron. D., & Schaeffer, J. (2007). Adolescents composing fiction in digital game and written formats: Tacit, explicit and metacognitive strategies. *E-Learning, 4*(3), 273-284.

New London Group (1996). A pedagogy of multiliteracies: Designing social futures. *Harvard Educational Review, 66* (1), 60-92.

Open University Team (2007, May). *The Schome-NAGTY Teen Second Life Pilot Final Report.* Retrieved October 18, 2008 from http://www.schome.au.uk

Provenzo, E. (1991). *VideoKids: Making sense of Nintendo.* Cambridge, MA: Harvard University Press.

Scott, K.A., Anderson, L., Zhang, X., Torrecillas, R., Chevalier, G., & Tyler, K. (2008, March). *COMPUGIRLS: Technology program for girls.* Workshop conducted at the Microcomputers in Education Conference, Tempe, AZ.

Steinkuehler, C. (2007). Massively multiplayer online gaming as a constellation of literacy practices. *E-Learning, 4*(3), 297-314.

Street, B. V. (1995). *Social literacies.* London: Longman.

Thomas, A. (2007). *Youth online: Identity and literacy in the digital age.* New York: Peter Lang.

Turkle, S. (1995). *Life on the screen: Identity in the age of the internet.* New York: Touchstone Books.

CHAPTER FOUR

Crossing Spaces of In-School and Out-of-School Literacies through Museum and Classroom Design, Production, and Consumption Practices

A. JONATHAN EAKLE

The purpose of this chapter is to report uses of museums in literacy education practices in and out of school, specifically those involving actual museums, simulated classroom museum experiences, and other virtual museums. These various uses of museums and the literacies that take place in, around, and about museums not only pass through various physical boundaries, such as classrooms and museum galleries, but also abstract and social ones. Lodged in these museum literacies are cultural values, textual multiplicities, design, production, and uses of texts, and their interrelations.

Museum texts, broadly defined to include images, printed labels, maps, gallery spaces, recorded and live oral scripts, and so forth, are aligned with principal concepts of the New Literacies movement and increasing complexities and interconnections of different modes of communicative meaning (The New London Group, 2000). In this vein, museum texts are not neutral but designed and produced for particular purposes and audiences, influence identity constructions, and involve power relations (Hooper-Greenhill, 2001; Karp & Levine, 1991; c.f., Collins & Blot, 2003; Street, 1984). And, for better or worse, the texts that are framed by museum architectures are often ones most valued by cultures.

In the following pages, first, I briefly trace the role of the virtual in various education and literacies domains. Then, in following sections uses of museums taken from three education research projects of museum and classroom design, production, and consumption practices involving literacies are described. These practices include new technologies and virtual environments as well as traditional ones, such as reading and writing printed texts, museum exhibitions, and school assignments that address education standards. Interspersed in these sections are resources for educators including references to online museum material. Further, a brief view of the complex of literacies and identity is provided through an examination of artists who were participants in one of the reported studies. I conclude with indications of museum literacies as catalysts for producing other education spaces and practices.

Virtual Spaces and Literacies

With the relatively new introduction of photography, cinema, television, and computer applications into everyday life during the past century, virtual spaces have taken on new meanings; the real and virtual sometimes crisscross almost indiscernible boundaries (Deleuze, 1986a, 1986b; Foster, 1999). At the extreme, hyper-realistic digital learning, such as virtual classrooms in online environments "where people are represented by avatars, classes are held on platforms in the sky and presentations are conducted in an amphitheatre" (Teachers College, 2008, n.p.) promises to someday become part of everyday life in education and being able to read and write virtual types of digital applications and preparing all students to engage in such literacies will likely be a charge of future educators.

Nonetheless, crisscrossing of the real and virtual is not the reserve of 21st century technologies. For instance, some printed texts can be portals to virtual spaces, such as Jorge Luis Borges' (1975) *Book of Sand*. The story is about a book whose print is ever changing and infinite and one and the same with a labyrinth, and of this labyrinth the *Book* surfaces in perhaps Borges' (1944/1998) most famous story, *Library of Babel*. Moreover, Borges' story does not end with printed text on a page. *The Book of Sand* has taken various twists and turns through readers' imaginations and also through other spaces, such as cinema and a hypertext puzzle where internet readers navigate Borges' labyrinth, complete with disappearing page numbers, moving illustrations, and random page orderings (Clarke, 2001). In short, many fine educators traverse similar spaces from the actual to the virtual through creative uses of imaginative teaching approaches, tools, and their productions of spaces, which can be as mundane as classroom learning centers that simulate real world activities, computer "screenlands" (Labbo, 1996, p. 356), or through escapes from typical school boundaries, such as museum activities that include actual and virtual spaces, as shown subsequently.

Creative productions of space are far from new to education, and a well-known example of this is the widely-debated "factory model" of schooling where children are sorted by age, regulated by bells, stamped by lessons valued by elders, held accountable by grading, among other means, and as a result are transformed to dedicated workers in mass (c.f., Leland, & Kasten, 2002; Ravitch & Viteritti, 1999). On the other hand, New Literacies theory and practices are counter to factory-like education approaches, yet, in a sense, draw from this model, by using key manufacturing terms such as design, production, and consumption (Cope & Kalantzis, 2000; Kress & van Leeuwen, 1996), but with awareness that we are situated in a postindustrial world that requires new creative designs, actions, perspectives, and products. A starting point is design, which in brief is the blueprint of what is produced, whether it is object, space, policy, or group and self-identity (Cope & Kalantzis, 2000), and it is also a critical launching point for examining literacies of larger networks of capital and flows that also includes production (e.g., of identities or objects) and consumption, such as reading various text forms and spaces. Likewise in this chapter notions of design, production, and consumption situate practices of literacies that are centered on: (a) museum text users and designers, such as students, teachers, museum curators, and artists, (b) museum products that draw from and can encourage imagination, and (c) actions and perspectives that can be cultivated through readily available old and new literacy objects and spaces, such as museum galleries, virtual online museums, and simulated classroom learning environments. Because of these uses and practices of various texts that are hinged to cultures, values, and identities, museums are rich sources from which the world can be read and written by people in and out of school.

Museum Literacies

Baroque paintings, gemstones, an enormous ball of string, and printed wall texts with facts about DNA share common ground as objects in popular museums. Further, museums are sites where various and sometimes competing cultural views are represented (Hooper-Greenhill, 2001; Karp & Levine, 1991). Annually, millions of visitors navigate diverse museum objects and exhibits using arrays of communicative resources. They read images, spaces, printed texts, engage with other media, and use language and movement, among other means, to learn and express museum content. Reading and expressing museum content, broadly defined to include diverse communication systems that consist of but are not limited to printed texts, are part and parcel of museum literacies.

Museums are extraordinary spaces where actual and virtual worlds often intersect. In recent years, I have explored these intersections and the literacies taken up by people in and around museum galleries and exhibitions. In part, this work involves how museum texts and spaces are designed and produced, and also how various people, such as classroom teachers and their students "consume," use, or do not use, museum literacies that they encounter.

Theories and Methods

The following sections of this chapter represent different studies involving museum literacies. Each of the studies used qualitative approaches, but each was framed with different, although overlapping, theoretical perspectives: (a) constructionist, (b) critical, and (c) poststructural. New Literacies viewpoints, such as design and redesigning, broadened definitions of texts, ideological text perspectives, and so forth influenced each of the investigations (e.g., Alvermann, 2002; Cope & Kalantzis, 2000; Street, 1984). For additional detail of how each study was conceptualized, readers may refer to cited works that follow.

In broad strokes, data collection methods of each study involved ethnographic tools and procedures: (a) participant observation recorded in field notes, (b) individual interviews (informal and formal semi-structured) conducted in various settings around schools, museums, and other spaces, and (c) the collection of documents and artifacts about the researched spaces. Further, during each study I made observational sketches, detailed drawings, and data maps and took photographs to record lengthy printed texts on museum and school walls, to supplement language text data, to capture lighting effects, flows of visitor movement, and so forth. In this vein, my data sets somewhat mirror museum gallery constructions.

Through some of this research I have shown how empirical data can be used to assemble literacies in a manner that presses against typical research frames and ways to display literacy education research. For example, taking notions and practices from contemporary digital video productions, in one study I created from verbatim dialog of participants, observations, images and other artifacts, and so on theatrical scenes spliced together to create various figures and situations. In addition, I fashioned "Special Features" that included Blockings, a term I borrowed from theatrical stage note procedures, Deleted Scenes, Outtakes, and Author Commentaries (Eakle, 2005, 2007a, 2007b).

These design-production approaches are aligned with concepts of assemblage and textual hybridization that appeared in fine art practices during the early 20th century, perhaps most famously through Cubism, and that threaded through Surrealism, Dada, 1960s ready-made art and continue on in various textual forms; assemblages are transformed from materials at hand, are intended to fracture conventional writing and other compositional space, to pass among notions and products of old and new communication forms, or literacies, and to operate with the intention of decentering authorial practice. "Materials at hand" were the stuff from which I drew, or "consumed," during my investigations, and once assembled and produced, or in other words published, were made available for further consumption by readers and so on. Again, cited works that follow provide further detail of data collection procedures and analyses and the different approaches I took in presenting respective studies.

Museum literacies: Designs, productions, and consumers

What happens in space, as Lefebvre (1974/2002) observed, "lends a miraculous quality to thought, which becomes incarnate by means of a design....The design serves as a mediator—itself of great fidelity between mental activity (invention) and social activity (realization)..." (pp. 27-28). In a similar vein, The New London Group (2000) laid out a multimodal, critical, meaning-making model wherein certain designing elements (e.g., gestural, visual, audio, and spatial) are blended in an attempt to understand and implement new literacies in new times that are used by "new people in new worlds" (Gee, 2002, p. 43). To be sure, spatial design and production as well as the design, production, and consumption of forms that occupy spaces are the stuff of new worlds, and also dated ones, for instance, fine arts of the past and those of contemporary institutions that display what is past, such as museums and other archives; these practices comprise portions of my education research in literacies, detailed subsequently.

Museum literacies of a second grade classroom

The first example of how museum literacies can be utilized is a rather conventional one involving a study of students' uses of various museum resources to produce a virtual museum in their second grade classroom (Eakle & Dalesio, 2008). Collaborating with Brooke Dalesio, a second grade classroom teacher in a Washington, DC, suburban school, we explored some of the possibilities of how a traditional classroom might take advantage of the multiple communication forms and means found in and through museums while addressing state education department standards. Further, underlying this project was the idea of opening spaces that allowed students to choose and assemble exhibited products in their classroom based on various topics of that interested them.

In a nutshell, the classroom activities were hinged to authentic literacy learning experiences, which initially involved students researching the roles of museum personnel, such as curators, public relations staff, and docents. They did so by reading printed texts about museum responsibilities, by visiting and interviewing employees in actual museums, and by exploring museum internet sites that included strolls through virtual realities, such as those of the White House Museum (2007). Extending from resources in the published article,

Table 4.1 provides samples of additional virtual museum internet sites that could be useful for the creation of similar activities.

Table 4.1 Samples of Exemplary Virtual Museum Learning Spaces

Museum	Selected Content	URL
Museum Stuff	Online directory of over 10,000 virtual museum sites	http://www.museumstuff.com/museums/
Museum of the Moving Image	1. Presidential campaign commercial archive (1952–present) 2. Online archive of award-winning short films created by young people about science and technology 3. Interactive tutorials of how motion pictures are designed and produced 4. Online catalog of over 2000 silent film era artifacts	http://www.movingimage.us/site/online/index.html
Marian Koshland Science Museum of the National Academy of Sciences	1. Streaming video of virtual exhibitions 2. Interactive multimedia, currently including: (a) "Infectious Diseases," (b) "Putting DNA to Work," (c) "Lights at Night," (d) "Global Warming Facts and Our Future," and (e) "Safe Drinking Water." 3. Teacher Resources and "Webquest Adventures" for students	http://www.koshlandsciencemuseum.org/exhibits/index.jsp
ArtMuseum.net	Project: Multimedia from Wagner to Virtual Reality (Online Video, printed hypertexts, and other multimedia of pioneers and exemplary practitioners of art/technology interfaces. Also included is an interactive teacher's guide)	http://www.artmuseum.net/w2vr/contents.html

Upon completing their research of the topics they selected, the students were invited to persuasively apply in writing for work roles in their virtual museum, a task that was aligned with state curriculum goals. Further, other authentic writing goals associated with creating the classroom museum were threaded through weeks of instruction. For instance, Writer's Workshop, a thirty-minute period set aside in the classroom each day, became a time when students researched and wrote about possible museum exhibition design and gallery content. Later these workshops centered on creating museum labels, descriptive exhibit texts, signs, and promotional materials, such as brochures to inform the school community and parents of the opening of the classroom museum. Alongside these somewhat traditional printed text-centered activities, participants also collected visual artifacts and other objects, digital materials, audio recordings, and so forth in designing their classroom museum exhibits from topics of their choice, which included musicians such as Elvis Presley, artists such as Monet, and topics about prehistoric life.

The virtual classroom museum was beneficial in meeting somewhat traditional school goals while employing new literacies and allowing students choices in the topics they researched. Particularly noteworthy were experiences and products of two students that we studied in detail. Jerry, identified by Brooke as a "high flying" student but one who had difficulty with social interactions at the onset of the school year was able to assume a classroom leadership role through the museum activities, and Mula Ken, who his teacher had described as a "determined struggler," was highly motivated by the museum project and developed conventional academic skills during the museum design and production and as a consumer of texts associated with his museum research (participant names and names of institutional spaces presented in this chapter are pseudonyms). Later in this chapter, I show how concepts from this article, among others, have been used in my graduate-level teacher education and literacy leadership classes.

Museum literacies in Mexico City

In a second qualitative research study conducted in Mexico City museums, Rosa Aurora Chávez-Eakle and I investigated the designing and production practices of three major museums (Eakle & Chávez-Eakle, under revision). One museum of the study was Arch Muse, an onsite archeology museum located in the excavated ruins of the principal ceremonial space of the Aztec Empire. It displays, and elaborates upon, artifacts taken from the surrounding excavation. Sci Muse, the second museum, is a hands-on science museum, and the third museum, Pop Muse, focuses on popular culture, specifically on products of rural and indigenous Mexican populations. We chose the three museums because of the diversity of their collections, their common missions of educating young people, and their prominence in Mexican culture. Of the latter, conducting multisite research of major institutions offers possibilities to study relations among local and global issues (Holmes & Marcus, 2005).

As part of this study, we focused on the work of three informants in the three different museums who were intimately involved in conceiving and orchestrating their respective museum's spaces. Across the sites, multiple communication modes, such as poetry, maps, printed texts, lighting effects, and pre-Hispanic codex composed of icons, ideographs, and symbols were designed and redesigned to produce museum space. Further, as in other museums introduced subsequently, the virtual was very much a part of the three museums we investigated. For instance, in Sci Muse there were simulated astronomy experiences, an exhibit where visitors could stroll through a gigantic book about the human body, and a tunnel that simulated the alimentary canal. Further, in the archeology museum galleries there were authentic Aztec objects but also detailed replicas of objects that remained in their original, unearthed contexts in the surrounding excavation. Such virtual reproductions of authentic historical objects by use of contemporary technologies, such as medical and other high resolution imaging, point to opportunities for "hands-on" explorations not only in museums, but also in schools.

Furthermore, through data from this study, we showed that to separate the designing and production of museum space from the wider context of Mexico City culture is tenuous, at best. For example, replete in the three museums were notions of Mexican identity and designed constructs of Mestizo hybridity, which reflect the melding of European and indigenous American cultures (Bonfil Batalla, 1996; Garcia Canclini, 1995/2001); for instance, the three museums were formed with concepts that celebrate Mexico's pre-Hispanic past while supported in part by, and situated within, a political and economic structure that has, and continues to alienate indigenous groups. The resulting fractured identity constructs mirror assemblages of the museums' designs, which involved complex ideological practices of economics and politics, such as printed texts explicitly denoting how identities have been fractured by occidental influences (e.g., pilfering of historic Mexican objects by colonizing outsiders) and also by ongoing neoconservative Mexican government policies. Concepts of fractured identities and blurred boundaries were also replete in other museums I have investigated, as shown in the following section of this chapter.

Because of the growing presence of students in the USA of Mexican heritage, drawing on museum resources of pre-Hispanic as well as more recent histories of Mexico, and so forth, could be useful in U.S. school practices for understanding some of the most profound aspects of Mexican cultures, what Bonfil Batalla (1996) described as *Mexico profundo*. To similar ends, presented

in Table 4.2, is a sample of Mesoamerican online resources that could contribute to teacher and teacher education activities and virtual classroom museums.

Table 4.2 Sample of Online Mesoamerican Resources

Website	Content	URL
Ancient Meso-american Civilizations	Numerous articles, photo-graphs, maps about Mixtec, Aztec, Zapotec, and Mayan cultures. Includes materials on Mesoamerican writing systems and calendars.	http://www.angelfire.com /ca/humanorigins/index.h tml
Museo Nacional de Anthroplogia	Three-dimensional rotatable images of Mesoamerican mu-seum pieces. Articles and other resources of Mexican cultures	http://www.mna.inah.gob .mx/muna/mna_ing/ main.html
Museo del Templo Mayor	Online flash movies involving major Aztec ceremonial center.	http://www.templomayor. inah.gob.mx/
Teaching Tolerance	Hundreds of teacher online re-sources about Latin American cultures and related issues. Free materials for teachers (e.g., teaching kits, such as "Viva la Causa" which includes DVD film about Cesar Chavez, teacher lesson plans, and other resources).	http://www.tolerance. org/

Museum literacies and artist identities
Spatial design and the designing of objects that occupy museum space is not
only the domain of museum curators, as in the museums touched on in the
previous section of this chapter, but also visual artists. Their spatial and visual
procedures and products are rich sources for studying intersections of literacies, and, as suggested earlier in this chapter, artists provide foundational

sources on how texts, broadly defined, have been taken from the ready-made, assembled from multiple sources, to create novel hybrid products. From this assumption, in research I conducted in classrooms and art museums in Marthasville, a Southeastern U.S. urban center (Eakle, 2005), I examined how visual artists took on central roles as designers and producers of museum texts, broadly defined. In part, the texts produced by the artists were oral ones that formed part of my data corpus, and as suggested in New Literacies theories, museum objects and spaces were open, continuous, and fluid. In following paragraphs, vignettes of two participating artists in the study are presented.

Blurred spatial boundaries were evident during the study through the destination of work created by Julia Jones, an artist informant in my research. I had met Julia while she was a "consumer" of an art exhibition in one of the museums I studied and recruited her as a participant. During an initial interview, she informed me that she was an artist. Julia had been awarded a commission by a regional airport, which sponsors a program that displays over 300 artworks rotating among concourses, and it also maintains permanent art exhibits and installations. The space is a mixture of virtual museum, actual travel, and commerce, among other things. I interviewed Julia as she was completing her airport art assemblage, which was to become a permanent installation there. It is a huge glass case filled with sequined white baby dresses on hangers, dolls, sewing buttons, and various sparkling objects. When asked about her design and production of the piece, Julia informed me:

> It's like conception and then it became a piece, a figure almost. There's an angel, there [pointing at the art piece] but it's a dress too...And there are buttons, I see buttons as connections to the spirit; you know, if we leave our bodies we still have our spirits, so I see a connection. And the button is very strong for me because mom was a seamstress...I don't know too much about her, just that she died having me, but these are some of the dresses she made and they are all white [gestures to the framed dresses in her art assemblage]. She made her own wedding dress, too...the piece there is very light. That's like the baby dresses, beginnings and light, but I think the womb without the young fetus is full of potential; it's dark; it's the height of dark, darkness, until the new life comes with light. To begin again. Ah.

As shown through Julia's words, the design/production of art texts can be intimately bound to artist identity and life events. So too was the sale of her art assemblage; she used most of the commission award to fix a large hole in the roof of her house. Presently, her mother's dresses hang in Julia's installation beside an airport escalator, advertising marquee, and coffee shop.

As with the airport, inside museums it is sometimes difficult to discern exhibition space from other spaces. Take, for instance, a gift shop at Carver House, one of the museums that I studied that displays art of Africa and African Diaspora. It was filled with work of regional artists: original images, sculp-tural forms reminiscent of those from Africa, jewelry, ceramics, and so forth. If price tags were removed from displayed pieces the shop could be mistaken for one of the museum's adjacent exhibit rooms.

On a table, there were small wooden boxes designed with printed texts, symbols, and other images. Typographies wrapped around and into the boxes, took on different languages, and blurred with other elements, such as photo-graphs. These pieces were created by Alem, a local artist and informant in the study. Alem identified with Ethiopian ancestry, and her appearance reflected her claim; her long dreadlocked hair was bound with a red, gold, and green head wrap, which also aligned her with Rastafari, a Jamaican group with ties to Pan African concepts and reggae music. Not only does Alem's art touch upon multiple modes and new literacies ideas, and also, as with Julia Jones' work, on self-identity concepts, which were reflected during an interview at the mu-seum:

> The misnomer is that we people of African descent don't read. I'm one of those peo-ple, earlier. Reading and comprehending was hard for me. Now, I read the particular things that are moving for me. I like to use reading in my art in a way that is not abrupt; so people can still get the information. It's like a reference card. You can see who the author is; you can go further, do research into those works. The boxes and other kinds of work I have are sort of like books. I visually describe something. They're kind of pictorial pieces, are like hieroglyphs, like books. The quote on this box is from His Imperial Majesty Emperor Haile Selassie and he wrote it, he made this speech on October 25, 1968, and I thought it was so interesting that even here in the United States with the constitution he would say [pointing to and reading from the box]: "All men are born free and equal invested in almighty God with unalienable human dignity..."
>
> JE [pointing to a corner of the box]: What's that word?
>
> Alem: That means "queen" in Amharic...It's Ethiopian.

As shown in this data snippet, Alem's opening remarks recount common myths and narratives of reading. Then, she transforms this line by describing her later engagement with *particular* text types, gathering and sharing text in-formation, and referencing. As well, there are identity traces in her comments. The speech she draws from is part of Rastafari narratives; Haile Selassie, who was an Ethiopian emperor, is regarded by them as a liberator of Africans and African Diaspora, groups upon which the Carver House museum focuses. Fur-ther, Alem's use of Amharic script is another identity marker; it is the national language of Ethiopia (Figure 4.1).

Figure 4.1. Sample Amharic Text (Courtesy of Ager, 2008)

የሰው ፡ ልጅ ፡ ሁሉ ፡ ሲወለድ ፡ ነጻና ፡ በክብርና ፡ በመብትም ፡ እኩልነት ፡ ያለው ፡ ነው ፡ የተፈጥሮ ፡ የማስተዋልና ፡ ሕሊናው ፡ ስላላው ፡ አንዱ ፡ ሌላውን ፡ በወንድማማችነት ፡ መንፈስ ፡ መመልከት ፡ ይገባዋል ።

The way that various language texts blurred on Alem's boxes is suggestive of the Tower of Babel from the biblical story of how people and languages were dispersed, a Rastafari theme, and it is also indicative of new literacies mixing and remixing procedures. In the following, Alem elaborated this line through words and gestures:

> Art is like a language... I don't think there is much difference between reading and looking at pictures...when you are reading, you're looking at little pictures that go together that make a sentence. Like all the "Ks" are just one line [in space, she gestures with her finger a vertical] and then you go here [gestures diagonals to complete an alphabetic K]. Writing is a minimalistic form of artwork.

Alem and Julia's assemblages of literacies were aligned with those of other artists in this same museum research project. For instance, as reported elsewhere (Eakle, 2007a), Lillian Johnson, an African American artist whose paintings appeared in a major Carver House Museum exhibition, also drew her imagery from language texts; "taken from a book, a scene from a book"; and she reported "There's a disjunction between visual images, because I want there to be that disjunction, because I want things to be uncomfortable...And that disjunction in itself gives it meaning" (p. 492).

Nonetheless, the disjunctive intent of Johnson's paintings led to assorted interpretations by other participants in the study. For instance, Ms. Jackson, a Christian faith-based middle school teacher, used Johnson's pictures to deliver a lesson to students about good and evil and the identities and differences of, as she described, "big G and little g" gods (p. 491). In comparison, Montsho, a museum docent, used the same images to teach lessons to visitors about "slave masters" and "African spirit washing up on the shores of America" (p. 488). And, reminiscent of Alem's assessment, Bishop, one of Ms. Jackson's adolescent students, stated: "The way I look at the [Johnson's] pictures is like reading, like I was right there, seeing what the artist was feeling...art is like a silent type of music..." (p. 490).

As shown in this section, indeed, designing, producing, and reading museum texts are tied to cultural and ideological points and values, sometimes intimately personal ones, tightly bound to identity constructions. As institutions that display what is often considered to be most valued by cultures, museums are rich sites for studying such complexes of literacies, identities, and values.

Furthermore, artists' assemblages, and descriptions of how they design and produce art works, can provide models for classroom practice. Consider, for instance, how a classroom museum literacies project, such as described earlier in this chapter (Eakle & Dalesio, 2008), might be designed to draw from personal aspects of students' lives, as was the case with Julia's art assemblage of baby dresses and other objects. Moreover, conceptual descriptions, inspirations, and products of artists point to alternative worlds that not only can engage certain audiences but also show that engagement with literacies may often be of the stuff found outside typical confines of formal education space, a focus of my research to which I now turn.

Museum literacies of adolescents "on their own"

To further explore out-of-school literacies, I examined data from an investigation of classrooms and art museums in the Southeastern United States (Eakle, 2005) to analyze how adolescents used museum literacies "on their own." For better or worse, young people are increasingly "on their own" and without adult supervision (Heath, 2000). And, more often than not they seek pleasurable ways to spend their time outside of the restraints of formal learning environments, such as factory-like schooling spaces mentioned earlier in this chapter. Museums, as informal learning institutions, offer possibilities as in-between spaces where young people can view domain-specific content, often related to material they encounter in schools, of their choice and at their own pace.

Targeted for extensive study were six adolescents in three out-of-school groups and two adolescents in a school group who chose to be "on their own" during museum fieldtrips. As reported elsewhere (Eakle, in press), a finding from the investigation was that participants rarely utilized, or otherwise "consumed," printed texts in a museum that specialized in arts of Greece, the Americas and Africa, although much expert care and expense had been taken by the museum to design and produce elaborate printed texts for visitors. In fact, the only significant printed text usage was by two girls as they played a decoding game in attempts to translate museum labels with "really long words," as one of the girls described it, and they poked fun at elaborate printed texts and labels, choosing only to look at museum displays.

Other adolescent participants "on their own" found further ways to have fun in the museum and to construct meaning from their experiences. For example, one group of boys strolled through the museum making connections among museum objects and activities and items from popular youth culture, such as anime and shooter video games, and another pair darted through museum spaces in imaginative play, pretending to be ancient rulers inside a virtual tomb labyrinth of the museum (Eakle, in press). Although not a novel concept, engaged, imaginative play, in these instances with museum spaces, deserves continued attention in formal education settings, not only in early childhood education play centers, but beyond.

Assuring for educators, when "on their own" in museums adolescents sometimes related literacies to material they had learned in school. For example, a detailed conversation occurred about a museum object from a recollection of a social studies unit, and upon seeing non-alphabetic script in a museum display, one participant reflected: "In Egypt they used pictures, you know, like how we use English and they change the words into pictures and different symbols way back in the day" (Eakle, in press), and in response to this statement another adolescent remarked that he had learned a bit of cuneiform in school. Indeed, museums, as with their precursor cabinets of curiosities, can foster imagination and stimulate or make enduring memories. Further, and as reported elsewhere (Eakle, 2007a) in between times of formal classroom instruction while "on their own" in schools, adolescents used content they had viewed in museums for their own purposes, which included constructing collages, notebook doodles, and freestyle rap lyrics incorporating and transforming exhibited museum concepts and objects. To be sure, museums can be springboards for multiple literacies. And, these student products reflect new literacies perspectives; things were selectively taken from the readily available in material culture, in this case and in part from museums, and transformed into products where authorship is distributed across time and space.

Museum Literacies as Catalysts for Creating Other Spaces

Through this chapter I presented a glimpse of multiple dimensions of possibilities for museum literacies in other learning contexts, such as literacy learning in schools. One facet touched on design and production practices in and of actual museums, and within this frame, how identity concepts and other personal aspects of literacies are embedded within such practices. Attention to how these qualities operate behind the scenes and on the surface of museums and through their literacies is important for educators to consider. Other features of this chapter addressed how museums can be rich sources for creating virtual learning spaces, such as in the second grade classroom, and how virtual digital museums, and the literacies found within those spaces, could be useful for various education purposes.

One purpose I have taken up as a teacher educator is the use of museum literacies as catalysts for literacy specialist candidates to explore education alternatives in a cross cultural studies course. The course assignments include:

(a) a "border crossing" experience where candidates research, engage in, and write about an unfamiliar and actual cultural environment, (b) reading and written online responses to peers involving *Reading Research Quarterly* articles written from four different theoretical perspectives, and readings from museum literacies research and New Literacies studies (e.g., Alvermann & Eakle, 2007; Eakle & Dalesio, 2008; Knobel & Lankshear, 2007), (c) a theory and research professional development group project where candidates explore in depth one of the four theoretical perspectives and then design and present their research to the whole class, and (d) meeting with a classroom teacher to discuss a curriculum-based classroom need and assisting the teacher in preparing an appropriate and realistic literacies lesson activity guided by The New London Group's (2000) multimodal design theories. The candidates use one of the four theoretical domains introduced in earlier course material to frame and design the lesson.

Using virtual museums in their lessons has been a popular choice for many of the candidates. Additionally, the design of virtual classroom museums has appealed to graduate students, and they have taken the lesson opportunity to initiate virtual museums in their schools, such as class-designed Wiki museums based on curriculum content. These activities often incorporate fieldtrips to actual museums abundant in our metropolitan area. Other candidates have been encouraged to design additional virtual spaces, including a virtual classroom zoo based, in part, on a fieldtrip to the National Zoo (a museum of sorts), and, in conjunction with an Earth Day celebration, the design and production of a school theater focusing on environmental issues.

Further, an ongoing project in a graduate student's school resulted from this set of course assignments: the design of a financial literacies initiative using New Literacies notions of design, production, and consumption of text materials based in financial and commercial markets in a fourth grade classroom where the teacher provided opportunities for students to create a virtual commercial space. Students worked with advertising concepts and images and designed and produced their own logos and slogans. They studied printed texts, engaged in virtual business scenarios, and explored business designs and ideas on the internet. Then, as a group they selected, designed, and implemented an actual reading tutoring "business" for first and second grade students in their school. In times of failing business on "Wall Street and Main Street," rising unemployment, and global economic challenges, financial literacies through virtual classroom design, production and consumer practices, as do museum literacies, could provide important possibilities for students to learn how to read and write critical aspects of their worlds.

Another purpose that museum literacies can serve in education settings is that as showcases of particular cultural values and texts that support such values, museums are ripe for deconstruction. This was apparent in the Mexican museums introduced earlier in this chapter and is also embedded in other museum spaces, such as ones lining the mall of the U.S. capital, a place of power, where artifacts taken from peoples are displayed, for example, those of North American tribes displaced by colonization. New Literacies and ideological notions of who produces texts and for what purposes are particularly salient in museums and in the hands of teachers and teacher educators can lead to illuminating activities of who we are, what is valued, who is marginalized, and what concepts and practices are sometimes dismissed.

Moving beyond school walls into museums also give educators and students sources and methods to possibly incorporate into their practices and everyday lives, for example, remixing and hybrid practices that have been benchmarks of the fine arts for over a century. Of the many examples populating museum corridors is the work of Joseph Cornell, a celebrated figure of assemblage who most notably created boxes containing found objects, which not only are available for viewing in actual museums but also in digital virtual spaces (see Pioch, 2002). Such practices of assemblage carried out and constructed from, and sometimes in opposition to, particular cultural values, can be exemplars for educators and their students to read, reread; write and rewrite their worlds, as was the case with local artists, museum designers, and adolescents described earlier in this chapter.

Absent from the preceding sections of this chapter was a finding across some of my studies: mostly school uses of museums were simply as fieldtrip destinations; unlike Eakle and Dalesio (2008), rarely did teachers prepare for or follow up on museum fieldtrips in their classroom instruction (Eakle, in press). Certainly, museums can be used for the instruction of academic content, and conventional, as well as newer forms of texts, could be touchstones for such practices. And, as shown through some of my work, museum literacies can be used to meet education standards through constructionist pedagogies. In this vein, the intersection of standards and museum literacies could provide some classroom teachers with escape routes to conserving and confining education mandates or could lead to disciplinary uses of museums by schools. Nonetheless, as suggested in this chapter through how some participants used museum spaces "on their own," appropriating museum literacies for conserving education purposes may be counter to some of the most imaginative and pleasurable aspects of museum visits, and operating at the margins of visibility and well outside mainstream education may be the greatest benefit of museum literacies.

References

Ager, S. (2008). *Amharic*. In Omniglot: Writing systems and languages of the world. Retrieved February 10, 2009 from http://www.omniglot.com/writing/amharic.htm

Alvermann, D. E. (Ed.). (2002). *Adolescents and literacies in a digital world*. New York: Peter Lang.

Alvermann, D. E., & Eakle, A. J. (2007). Dissolving learning boundaries: The doing, re-doing, and undoing of school. In D. Thiessen & A. Cook-Sather (Eds.), *International handbook of student experience in elementary and secondary school* (pp. 143-166). Dordrecht, The Netherlands: Springer.

Bonfil Batalla, G. (1996). *México profundo: Reclaiming a civilization* (P. A. Dennis, Trans.). Austin, TX: University of Texas Press.

Borges, J. L. (1975). *The book of sand* (N.T. Giovanni, Trans.). Retrieved February 10, 2009 from http://artificeeternity.com/bookofsand/

Borges, J. L. (1998). The tower of Babel. In *Jorges Luis Borges, Collected fictions* (A. Hurley, Trans.) (pp. 112-118). New York: Penguin. (Originally published 1944)

Clarke, M. (2001). *The book of sand. A hypertext puzzle*. Retrieved January 5, 2009 from http://artificeeternity.com/bookofsand/

Collins, J., & Blot, R.K. (2003). *Literacy and literacies: Texts, power, and identity*. Cambridge: Cambridge University Press.

Cope, B., & Kalantzis, M. (Eds.). (2000). *Multiliteracies: Literacy learning and the design of social futures*. London: Routledge.

Deleuze, G. (1986a) *Cinema 1: The movement-image* (H. Tomlinson and B. Habberjam, Trans.). Minneapolis: University of Minnesota Press. (Originally published in 1983)

Deleuze, G. (1986b). *Cinema 2: The time image*. Minneapolis, MN: University of Minnesota Press. (Originally published 1989)

Eakle, A. J. (2005). *Literacy in the art museum: A theatre of values*. Unpublished doctoral dissertation. The University of Georgia, Athens.

Eakle, A. J. (2007a). Literacies spaces of a Christian faith-based school. *Reading Research Quarterly, 42,* 472-511.

Eakle, A. J. (2007b). Museum literacy, art, and space study. In D. Lapp, J. Flood, & S. B. Heath (Eds), *Handbook of research on teaching literacy through the communicative and visual arts* (2nd Ed.), (pp.179-188). Mahwah NJ: Lawrence Erlbaum.

Eakle, A. J. (2008). *Figures, rings, and escape lines: Using the logic of sensation and art in conducting, deconstructing, and assembling literacy education research*. Paper presented to the 58th annual National Reading Conference. Orlando, Florida.

Eakle, A. J. (In Press). Museum literacies and adolescents using multiple forms of texts "on their own." *Journal of Adolescent & Adult Literacy*.

Eakle, A. J. & Chavez-Eakle, R. A. (under revision). Museum literacies in Mexico City: An examination of texts, spaces, and practices of expert designers.

Eakle, A. J., & Dalesio, B. (2008). Museum literacies in a second grade classroom. *The Reading Teacher, 61*(8), 604-613.

Foster, H. (1999). *The return of the real: The avant-garde at the end of the century.* Cambridge, MA: MIT Press.

Garcia Canclini, N. (2001). *Consumers and citizens: Globalization and multicultural conflicts* (G. Yudice, Trans.). Minneapolis: University of Minnesota Press. (Originally published 1995)

Gee, J. P. (2002). Millennials and bobos, *Blue's Clues* and *Sesame Street*: A story of our times. In D. E. Alvermann (Ed.), *Adolescents and literacies in a digital world* (pp. 51-67). New York: Peter Lang.

Heath, S.B. (2000). Making learning work. *After School Matters,1*, 33-45.

Holmes, D. R. & Marcus, G. E. (2005). Refunctioning ethnography: The challenge of an ethnography of the contemporary. In N. K. Denzin and Y.S. Lincoln (Eds.), *The Sage handbook of qualitative research* (3rd Ed.) (pp. 1099-1113). Thousand Oaks, CA: Sage Publications.

Hooper-Greenhill, E. (2001). *Museums and the interpretation of visual culture.* London: Routledge.

Karp, I. V. & Levine, S. D. (1991). (Eds.). *Exhibiting cultures: The poetics and politics of museum display.* Washington, DC: Smithsonian.

Knobel, M., & Lankshear, C. (2007). *A new literacies sampler.* New York: Peter Lang.

Kress, G., & van Leeuwen, T. (1996). *Reading images: The grammar of visual design.* London: Routledge.

Labbo, L.D. (1996). A semiotic analysis of young children's symbol making in a classroom computer center. *Reading Research Quarterly, 31*, 356-385.

Lefebvre, H. (2002). *The production of space* (D. Nicholson-Smith, Trans.). Oxford, UK: Blackwell. (Original work published 1974)

Leland, C. H., & Kasten, W. C. (2002). Literacy education for the 21st century: It's time to close the factory. *Reading and Writing Quarterly, 8*, 5-15.

The New London Group (2000). A pedagogy of multiliteracies: Designing social futures. In B. Cope and M. Kalantzis, (Eds.), *Multiliteracies: Literacy learning and the design of social futures* (pp. 9-37). London: Routledge.

Pioch, N. (2002). *Joseph Cornell. WebMuseum, Paris* [online]. Retrieved February 15, 2009 from http://www.ibiblio.org/wm/paint/auth/cornell/

Ravitch, D. & Viteritti, J. D. (1999). New York: The obsolete factory. In D. Ravitch and J. D. Viteritti (Eds.), *New schools for a new century* (pp. 17-36). New Haven, CT: Yale University Press.

Street, B.V. (1984). *Literacy in theory and practice.* London: Cambridge University.

Teachers College (2008). *Technology initiatives @ TC: Second Life.* Retrieved January 5, 2009 from http://www.tc.columbia.edu/cis/techinit.asp?Id=Technology+Initiatives+@+TC&Info=Second+Life

The White House Museum (2007). [Online] Retrieved January 5, 2009 From http://www.whitehousemuseum.org/

CHAPTER FIVE

Day of Tears: Day of Desperation
Using Blogging to Make Social Studies Content Engaging and Comprehensible

MELISSA I. VENTERS

Whether we like it or not, technology plays a significant role in the lives of the students we teach. Adolescents, looking for new ways of communicating, networking, and circulating information, have turned to the use of technological webblogs. A Weblog, the official term for blog, is defined as a personal website that provides updated headlines and news articles of other sites that are of interest to the user and may also include journal entries, commentaries and recommendations compiled by the user (Dictionary.com, 2008). Blogs are often characterized as online journals that are regularly updated with brief postings (Merchant, 2006). Most blog posts are textual, and many also contain images, photos, hypertext links to other sites, and allowance for audience comments. Some examples of popular Weblogs among adolescents include MySpace (www.myspace.com) and Facebook (www.facebook.com). On these sites, users share identities they produce of themselves through pictures and videos they post, thoughts they write and update often, and other items they find worthy to include. They not only share information about themselves, but they also use the technology to learn about others' identities as they navigate pages created by their friends. The time spent on these websites helps adolescents engage in social networking practices that are central to their day-to-day lives (Williams & Merton, 2008).

According to recent research on adolescents, at least 8 million adolescents blog (Kornblum, 2005). A Pew Internet Study (Berson & Berson, 2006) found that 57% of the twenty-one million adolescents that use the internet have contributed content to the web, and 19% of them have created their own blog. Furthermore, more than half of all blogs are maintained by people ages 13-19 (Magid, 2006).

Although adolescents' out-of-school literacies include online life for social networking (Williams & Merton, 2008) and for the chronicling of their current lives (Richardson, 2006), most students find the school content of social studies to be the least liked subject and of less importance when compared to other subjects (Stodolsky, Salk & Glaessner, 1991). Within a lecture-driven delivery system of content, most students in the United States find social studies to be the least interesting of subjects in the school curriculum (Shaughnessy & Haladyna, 1985). A stark contrast then is set between the social networking of adolescents' out-of-school lives and the individualized, passive acceptance of social studies content in their in-school lives. Perhaps by connecting blogging, which is such an integral part to many students' out-of-school literacies, to school content, student engagement, understanding, and uses of social studies will improve.

In this chapter, I report on my implementation of an action research project of using new literacies, and specifically weblogs with eighth graders, to invigorate the social studies curriculum by connecting content to their interest in blogging. First, I review the relevant research on new literacies and blogging. Then I lay out the methodology, classroom implementation, and unit of study. Lastly, I analyze the findings and share classroom implications and instructional considerations.

Related Research

Because students in many social studies classes fail to see the connections between social studies and their own lives, and quite possibly because some teachers fail to show them those connections, students tend to have varying degrees of apathy toward the subject. In an effort to combat student apathy, to increase student motivation, to invigorate the curriculum with content relevant to students' lives, some teachers have turned to new literacies to learn about adolescents' interests in and uses of new forms of communication.

New literacies have been defined as those literacies that have emerged in the post-typographic era (Semali, 2001) and may not be new at all but new to the context in which they are used (Lankshear & Knobel, 2003). These include, but are certainly not limited to, making content relevant by using media such as technology, music, popular magazines, and comics, to name a few. Some research has examined pedagogical frameworks of new literacies and adolescents' uses of new literacies in schools (cf. Hagood, Skinner, Venters, & Yelm, 2009; Hagood, Provost, Skinner, & Egelson, 2008). Abadiano &Turner (2007), Hagood (2000), and Semali (2001) described this pedagogical framework in their writings. Hagood (2000) described instruction using new literacies as a critical content in teacher education preparation for the new millennium, and all these researchers agree that technology and media are priorities of teacher education practices that attempt to keep up with these technologically changing times.

Hagood, Provost, Skinner, and Egelson (2008) implemented new literacies strategies in English language arts and social studies content areas over a two-year period in two underperforming middle schools. The strategies used in these schools included uses of media such as MovieMaker, comics, raps, movies, and blogging as means to understand students' uses and comprehension and to connect to the English and social studies content. I participated in this study as a classroom teacher, learned about blogging as a form of educational strategy to engage students, and developed my own action research project using blogging as the means for students to craft ideas and arguments about their thinking on social studies standards related to South Carolina history and the Civil War.

Middle school classrooms can embrace blogs and use them as a tool to increase student engagement, understanding, and motivation. Blogging and its potential to support learning have been the subject of some research and writing. Abadiano and Turner (2007) found that literacy instruction is enhanced by blogging, partially due to the social networking capability blogging affords. Student blogging also creates an increased sense of student empowerment by allowing students to take ownership (Ferdig & Trammell, 2004). Additionally, Carlson (2003) discovered that blogging generates increased collaboration and interaction, enhances opportunity for student feedback, and extends learning outside the classroom among college students.

Some research has shown improvement in science, math, and English content when students use blogging. Luehmann and MacBride (2008) concluded that blogging was in fact effective in high school math and science classrooms. They found that many of the adolescent participants went beyond the required number of blog entries and participated in the blog in unprecedented numbers. Not only that, but students' motivation within the classroom, including participation and engagement, increased as well.

Noticeably absent from the literature, however, are the benefits of classroom blogging in the *social studies* classroom. New literacies in the area of blogging hold potential for social studies educators as a means to make more enagaging what is often considered the most boring subject to adolescents' way of thinking.

New literacies, and specifically the uses of blogging, have potential to fit almost flawlessly with what social studies education strives to accomplish. In *Teaching History for the Common Good*, Barton and Levstik (2004) outlined core principles of social studies education that seek to prepare students for a democratic society. First, they insist that students serve as active agents in learning, which blogging would certainly generate. Second, they maintain that students need a humanistic education, one in which they identify with the past, learn lessons from it, and gain a sense of historical empathy. Further, the

Task Force on Social Studies in the Middle School (Levy et al., 1991) set forth ideals for social studies education. These ideals include concern for the development of self-identity, development of ethical stances, and concern for the world. Alignment between instruction and content delivery using student blogging may well assist in the development of these ideals.

Methodology

In order to gage the effectiveness of reflective blogging in the middle school social studies classroom, I used a qualitative research approach (Marshall & Rossman, 1999). Data collection included observations of students' use of a teacher-directed blog, artifacts of students' blog entries, anecdotal notes written after informal interviews of students' perceptions of the project, and student checklists that held records of student work.

Westview Middle (a pseudonym) is an urban school located approximately five miles outside of downtown Charleston, South Carolina. The middle school itself consists of a majority of African American students and a minority of Latino, Asian, and White American students. The school includes grades six through eight, and 69% of the students are on free or reduced-priced lunch, qualifying it as a Title One school. The school was rated as "unsatisfactory" on the South Carolina Report Card in 2006 and 2007, reflective of the students' low statewide assessment scores. Because of this negative and below average rating, teachers at the school feel constant pressure from administration to raise end-of-year test scores. As a failing school, the school district selected Westview to participate in a two-year study of the implementation of new literacies strategies in English and social studies content areas across the three grades. Therefore, much of my classroom instruction included combining new literacies with course content, often in relation to preparation of students for state testing.

I received an undergraduate degree in history and secondary education, and I am currently working on a graduate degree in social studies. As an eighth grade South Carolina History teacher, I taught all levels of social studies to eighth graders during the 2007-2008 school year (honors, general, resource, and self-contained). I taught a total of six classes, seeing three classes a day, and each class being ninety minutes in length. Approximately half of my students scored "Below Basic" as seventh graders on the social studies portion of the PACT (Palmetto Achievement Challenge) year-end standardized state test, making it extremely critical to use unique methods of teaching content to students to engage them and to increase their understanding and retention of content.

Classroom Implementation

Day of Tears (Lester, 2004) is historical fiction. The story is set in Savannah, Georgia, during the antebellum period, and it is written about the real-life events of the largest slave auction in United States history, that of Pierce Butler's slaves (see http://www.pbs.org/wgbh/aia/part4/4p1569.html for more information on Pierce Butler's life). The eighth grade team of teachers chose *Day of Tears* for several reasons. First, the book connected emotionally with students and evoked a sense of empathy/sympathy and compassion towards the subject of slavery as it covered the perspectives of slaves, slave owners, and abolitionists in the story. Second, the book is written in the third-person omniscient voice, containing several narrators and different and complex perspectives of whites and blacks towards the issue of slavery. This format was useful not only as a means for teaching students the concept of voice, but it also gave teachers and students a common text for analyzing racial issues. Lastly, as historical fiction, this novel sparked student interest, as the teaching about the history of slavery is part of the South Carolina state standards, and historic plantations—now museums—are within ten miles of the school.

This interdisciplinary unit approach (see Table 5.1) included the teamwork of teachers of eighth grade social studies, reading, and writing, and also two resource teachers for students with learning disabilities, a teacher for students with emotional and mental disorders, and the teacher who addressed reading remediation. Seven teachers shared sixty copies of the book among their students throughout the implementation of the project. The teacher team met during both common planning time and before and after school and emailed regularly in order to communicate openly about the successes and challenges of the project.

Day of Tears was read by all eighth grade students and took approximately one month to read in class. Automated reading (Samuels, 1979) was used to assist students who had difficulty reading the book independently. These students listened to an audio compact disc while following along in the book. Discussions, activities, and projects were interspersed between the reading of the book.

Content related to slavery, a central strand of South Carolina standards, was taught through the social studies class, as part of a larger discussion on the Civil War. Related topics covered included: causes of the Civil War, perspectives of the North and South, connection between slavery and the war, and Reconstruction. *Day of Tears* fit perfectly, bringing the history text to life for the students, as it addressed all of these areas.

Table 5.1 Interdisciplinary Unit Plan for Day of Tears

Content	Assessments
Primary Text: *Day of Tears* (Lester, 2004) Secondary Text: Media suggestions: "Still I Rise" (Angelou, 1994) Cold content reading of Weeping Time (n.d.) Educational version of *Glory* (1989) Selected scenes from *Shawshank Redemption* (1994)	Journals Weekly blogging Class discussions Debates Differentiated tests Common assessment across content areas: Friendly letter
Enduring Understandings/Objectives and Essential Questions	

- Students will be able to identify and write about the universal themes in the novel such as: hope, desperation, solidarity, and endurance.
- What do metaphors like "tears" and "rain" symbolize throughout the book?
- How does Lester's novel in dialogue humanize this time period? What makes it different from the secondary sources we've studied?
- How is slave culture depicted throughout the novel?
- What events led up to or triggered this time period?
- What connections can we make between this time period and SC culture now?
- How were African Americans exploited not only through slavery but also through the Civil War and Reconstruction?

The blogging portion of the project using *Day of Tears* occurred during students' social studies classes. The blog was set up on www.classblogmeister. com. This was the only blog site available to students at school, as all others were blocked by the district-wide computer filter. The blog included five reflective comprehension areas and links to websites relating to slavery and the real-life characters in *Day of Tears*. Students posted reflections needed to follow Bloom's Revised Taxonomy (Marzano & Kendall, 2006) at the levels of comprehension, application, analysis, synthesis, and evaluation. Setting up the blog to post responses in this format incorporated the components of a different school-wide initiative for improved instruction to meet students' educational needs. This response format, in turn, served as a means of differentiating the blogging in order to meet the needs of the many different student learning levels. Student blogging counted as a project grade, which was twenty percent of their end-of-quarter social studies grade.

To introduce students to the project and to activate their schema about the content of the book, I taught several initial lessons. In a blog introductory lesson, students received background knowledge of the true-life events that inspired the writing of *Day of Tears*. I explained to the students that, through the use of historical fiction, *Day of Tears* illustrated the real life "weeping time," that day that Pierce Butler held the largest slave auction in American history. I included links to web sites, explaining the events of this historical occasion on the blog, so students could browse them at their leisure. Students also received blog directions/instructions and were taught how to use the blog in order to complete their project (see Table 5.2). This lesson included using a Smartboard to model for students the blog and how to navigate the blogmeister website using detailed directions and instructional handouts, which students followed during independent practice.

Table 5.2 Blog Directions for Day of Tears

Directions: You will use the blog to reflect on the reading of *Day of Tears*. You must answer and participate in at least 3 of the blog reflective prompts.

1. Go to www.classblogmeister.com
2. Go to "select state" and put in South Carolina.
3. You will be asked to "select a teacher." Find "Venters, Melissa" and click.
4. You will see the 5 blog reflective prompts in the middle of the page. Choose which prompt you wish to answer and click on "comment."
5. Then click "add a comment."
6. Type in your name and your comment.
7. Enter the correct letters and numbers in the box entitled "Prove that you're a human!"
8. Finished! I will approve your entry, and then it will post.

There are 5 blog prompts you may respond to. They are:
1. Evaluation: We have discussed slavery MANY TIMES in social studies class. Identify and describe 3 things from the book that relate to what we have learned in social studies class. Include page number(s).
2. Synthesis: Throughout the novel, the word "rain" is used as a metaphor that compares rain to the oppression and hopelessness felt by the characters. Create another metaphor that could be used throughout this novel in the place of "rain." Defend your use of this word.
3. Comprehension: Some of the characters in this novel will surprise you when you learn of their position toward slavery. Identify the positions of 2 characters in this novel toward slavery. Were they pro (for) or anti (against) and how to you know this?
4. Application: While reading this novel, you will encounter several powerful words and/or sentences that will really make you think. Identify and describe one such instance and remember to give the page number(s) where these powerful words/sentences can be found.
5. Analysis: While reading this novel, the reader is expected to feel many emotions, especially anger and sadness. Identify and explain something that really made you mad and/or sad in the novel. Make sure to give the page number(s) where this information can be located.

Continued on next page

Table 5.2 continued

How and when are you going to do this?
• You will have some time in social studies and your reading/writing teachers may also allow you some class time.
• You may use the back of this paper as a rough draft. Have it out when you are reading the book in reading class. You may want to jot things down while you are reading.
• BE RESPONSIBLE: You may blog as much as you want, but I will only grade the required 3 blog responses. Think before you write…do not go crazy with the blogging ☺
• EXTRA CREDIT: You may also respond to others' comments for extra credit.

Students had five weeks to blog responses at least three times while reading *Day of Tears*. They had to blog responses related to teacher-directed prompts, but they could also write responses to peers' blog postings they read. Based upon the blog entry settings on the website, I had to accept or decline students' entries before they posted to the site for others to read. Some students used time during social studies and reading classes to complete the required entries; other students chose to blog at home. Blog postings were graded based upon adequate completion using a student checklist I created.

Findings and Analysis of Student Blogging

With the execution of student blogging, student engagement increased dramatically compared to other assignments and projects given throughout the school year. Eighty-five percent of the students completed all three required blog postings, and 23% percent of the students received extra credit for completing more than the three required blog posts. Many students informally noted that they either wrote or read blogs outside of school. Therefore, most of the students were already familiar with blogging and were more willing to participate. Students found the project more connected to their everyday lives as they were able to log on and write, much like they do outside of school. Connecting students' out-of-school interest with an in-school assignment, albeit teacher controlled, seemed favorable to students' interest and engagement.

Students were allowed the opportunity not only to engage in social networking by connecting with their peers in this blogging space, but their understanding and comprehension of interdisciplinary content were also enhanced within this space of the unit study. This content met the requirements of the South Carolina state standards that students would likely see on their end-of-the-year state testing. The first response area of the blog guided students to compare content from the book to social studies content covered in class. Students who answered this prompt had to draw comparisons and to use social studies content to defend their stances. An example of the types of blog answers given follows:

> Many times in South Carolina History our class has discussed how slaves were treated {slave conditions}. We read about how masters would beat there slaves for doing nothing or accusing them of doing something. This relates to *Day of Tears* because on page 122-124 is Sampson's Interlude he tells about the first plantation he was on before Master Heniefield saved him. He tells about how he got cracked with a whip because the overseer thought he did something. (February 2008)

Slave conditions and the relationships between different classes and races on plantations were an important aspect of slavery content taught in social studies class. As this example shows, students made clear connections between excerpts from the book and content standards that needed to be retained.

Some blogging discussions touched on deep and personal content, and students made connections between standards, the book, and their personal views. One such reflection prompt that elicited these sorts of answers asked students to identify two characters in the book as either pro-slavery or anti-slavery and defend their answer. An example of a student blog answer follows:

> Well the slave owner is pro-slavery. One he thinks that n*****s don't have feelings. Another way you know is he says that he doesn't have any sympathy for a man who has feelings for n*****s. He wanted to join the Ku Klux Klan and he wanted a reputation of giving the best deals in slave auctions. He's a racist and he admits to doing horrible things to the African community. Another person who is pro-slavery is Frances. Mr. Butler's daughter is pro-slavery, because she can't wait to get the plantation. When her father dies she gets the plantation, slaves, and everything else. She did just that, and married a man who was pro-slavery. She treated Emma like she was property and loved the idea of slavery. She just wanted to get closer to her father and get attention. Those are the two positions in which both characters are (pro) for slavery. (February 2008)

Throughout the first semester of social studies class, students explored people's feelings about slavery. Through defining "pro-slavery" and "anti-slavery" in class and then reading the voices of people who supported these views in *Day of Tears*, students better understood and explained their positions toward slavery. Furthermore, by blogging, they shared their ideas in a different, informal way. Because students could think about and write their responses, they were able to perhaps share information quite differently than had they been expected to explain their views during a discussion in class.

Blogging also proved beneficial in understanding content and standards relative to their English and writing classes. For example, students were asked to create another metaphor for the word "rain" used throughout the novel. Students' understanding of figurative language improved as they wrote about and synthesized their own metaphors. One student used the metaphor "asthma," as explained below:

> The characters in the novel experienced a lot of pain and the author used rain to describe the intensity of their pain. Like having an asthma attack the intensity of trying to breath is like the intensity of their pain because they could not be freely express their feelings of hurt, disappointment, or deceit. (February 2008)

What was most surprising about this student's response was that this was a girl who was in her first year of regular, mainstreamed classes. In prior years, she was in a self-contained class for students with emotional disabilities. Her reading comprehension was significantly below eighth grade level. Yet by reading the novel in class and participating in the blog, she increased her understanding of both social studies and English content.

One area that developed across social studies and English/language arts content was the concept of understanding authorial "voice" and using "voice" in blogging. Students identified with the concept of *voice*, an important term in literature, as the novel is narrated by several people. Rather than reading a book that presents a story through one narrator, *Day of Tears* showed students how an individual's voice can change the tones and perspectives of an event or story. Through the use of different narrators, students gained a sense of their own voices, which they utilized in their blogging. One such example resulted from the blog prompt that asked students to explain powerful words/sentences that they encountered in the novel:

> On page 47 when master Pierse is about to die he say why would people want to go to war over African American slaves. Also that if there was no slavery would you(whites) want them(blacks) living next door to them and marrying their daughters. Also going to school with whites. I found this comment very offensive even thow i am not black. It is offensive to me because some of my best friends are black. this statement also made me feel disipointed in white history and it made me angry. (February 2008)

Another example of student understanding of and use of voice in their blogs is when students were asked to describe their emotions while reading this novel. Two student responses follow:

> This book makes me feel angry in some ways and sad in others. I feel angry about the way the slave seller acts throughout the story. He acts ignorant. He treats slaves like their a piece of trash but makes all this money off of them. So if it wasn't for the pieces off trash he's selling, he'd be nothing. Pierce Butler ain't nothing better than that whispering bum. He sits there and feels sorry for himself because he's wack at the card table. He talks about how he feels sorry for the slaves that he has to sell them. Thats a load of crap. If you were so kind-hearted and sorry for them, why'd you buy them!!! I also feel kind of sad because how Emma gets split up from her family. I

know that if I got split up from my family, I probally wouldn't be nothing. But what made it all worse was how Master Butler went back on his promise to Will and Mattie. (February 2008)

The one thing that made me mad was the "n" word. Why do they use that word so much. When I hear that word, it makes me want to react. I found that word on pgs. 28,31,32x2,33,39,47x5,782,91,96,97,105,108,120,123x4,124x3,128,140x2,141x2,15 3,and 154. That is all the pages I found that word on. (February 2008)

Students were motivated to answer these two prompts in particular, because they were able to state their opinions and to express their emotions regarding some of the heavier, more provocative components of the novel. Furthermore, students overheard each other discussing their entries, and they often read each others' entries before they wrote their own. Because they posted their writing on the blog, they were aware that they had an audience of peers much larger than just a single teacher reading their thoughts, and they used their reach to make their points such that they engaged in a form of social networking as part of their online answers to the questions.

Classroom Implications and Instructional Considerations

Although school data suggested that standardized test scores improved little after the completion of this project, other benefits resulted from using blogging in the social studies classroom. First, student engagement greatly improved. Students were excited about blogging and willingly completed the assignment. Their sense of ownership and interest in the project decreased many of the negative behaviors sometimes found among the students who were normally categorized as underperforming. Furthermore, students had fewer absences during this project, and more students completed this project than any other social studies project during the year.

Although the team took a great deal of time to lay the groundwork for this interdisciplinary unit, several issues and challenges arose that are worthy of consideration before implementing such a project again. First, all eighth graders were not included in the culminating writing assessment, which addressed the state standard of writing a friendly letter using the writing process to produce a polished and finished piece of writing. Only those students in honors, general, and resource writing class completed the friendly letters, excluding students who were in self-contained reading remediation classes. These are the students that may have benefited the most from a common culminating assessment. Second, only having sixty copies of Day of Tears proved to be a challenge. Instead, it would have been more beneficial for each of the seven teachers implementing the project to have a class set of the book. Third, a more challenging book could have been used for more advanced students. Examples of such works of historical fiction include *Copper Sun* (Draper, 2008) and *Uncle Tom's Cabin* (Stowe, 2004). Fourth, in order to assist students in gaining a better understanding of the real voice of slaves, works of nonfiction, such as *To Be a Slave* (Lester, 2005), could have served as companion texts to *Day of Tears*. And finally, the blog site I used was more labor intensive than I expected. Because of the school district filter on all computers at the school I was limited by the blog site selection. The particular site forced me to accept each student's entry before posting. Consequently, I narrowed the focus of the project by directing the students' blogging by answering teacher-directed reflective prompts. Although students could post entries outside of the designated topic questions, none of them did so, mostly because they had to wait for me to clear their entries before posting.

Through this project I found that in order to reach adolescents in classrooms, especially those in high-poverty, underperforming schools, teachers need to appreciate and connect the literacies of students' lives to the content taught. Social studies content, traditionally seen by students of all ages as boring and unimportant, could particularly heed the advice of researchers and integrate the use of teacher-directed student blogging. This may not only prove to increase the engagement and motivation in students but may also increase the understanding of content and literature relative to the material covered in class.

Author's note: I thank Chandler Dabit and Lisa Hayes, both middle school educators, for the assistance they provided with the development and implementation of the unit. I also thank Margaret Hagood, a College of Charleston professor, for the assistance and guidance provided for the construction of this chapter.

References

Abadiano, H. R., & Turner, J. (2007). New literacies, new challenges. *The New England Reading Association Journal*, 43(1), 75-8.

Angelou, M. (1994). *The complete collected poems of Maya Angelou*. New York: Random House.

Barton, K., & Levstik, L. (2004). *Teaching history for the common good*. London: Lawrence Erlbaum Associates.

Berson, I.R., & Berson, M.J. (2006). Privileges, privacy, and protection of youth bloggers in the social studies classroom. *Social Education, 70* (3), 124-129.

Carlson, S. (2003). Weblogs come to the classroom. *The Chronicle of Higher Education*, 50(14), A33.

Draper, S. (2008). *Copper sun*. New York: Simon & Schuster.

Ferdig, R. & Trammell, K. (2004). Content delivery in the blogosphere. *The Journal Online*, 31(7), 12-20.

Fields, F. (Producer), & Zwick, E. (Director). (1989). *Glory* [Motion Picture]. United States: TriStar Pictures.

Hagood, M. (2000). New times, new millennium, new literacies. *Reading Research and Instruction*, 39, 311-328.

Hagood, M.C., Provost, M., Skinner, E., & Egelson, P. (2008). Teachers' and students' literacy performance in and engagement with new literacies strategies in underperforming middle schools. *Middle Grades Research Journal 3(3)*, 57-95.

Hagood, M. C., Skinner, E., Venters, M., & Yelm, B. (2009). New literacies and assessments in middle school social studies content area instruction: Issues for classroom practices. In A. Burke and R. F. Hammett (Eds.), *Assessing new literacies: Perspectives from the classroom* (pp.75-91). New York: Peter Lang.

Kornblum, J. (2005, October 30). Adolescents wear their hearts on their blogs. *USA Today*. Retrieved http://www.usatoday.com/tech/news/techinnovations/2005-10-30-adolescent-blogs_x.htm.

Lankshear, C. & Knobel, M. (2007). *A new literacies sampler*. New York: Peter Lang.

Lester, J. (2004). *Day of tears: A novel in dialogue*. New York: Hyperion Books.

Lester, J. (2005) *To be a slave*. New York: Puffin Books.

Levy, T., Altoff, P. Hannum, L., Haskvitz, A., Miller, M., Mouldon, R., & Nikell, P. (1991). *Social studies in the middle school: A report of the task force on social studies in the middle school*. Retrieved from http://www.socialstudies.org/positions/middleschool/.

Luehmann, A., &. MacBride, R. (May 2008). Capitalizing on emerging technologies: A case study of classroom blogging. *Science and Mathematics, 108,* 173-183.

Magid, L. (2006). Adolescent guide to safe blogging. Retrieved from http://www.blogsafety.com/thread.jspa?threadID=1200000051.

Marshall, C., & Rossman, G.B. (1999). *Designing qualitative research.* Thousand Oaks, CA: Sage.

Marvin, N. (Producer), & Darabont, F. (Director). (1994). *Shawshank Redemption* [Motion Picture]. Hollywood: Castle Rock Entertainment.

Marzano, R., & Kendall, J. (2006). *The new taxonomy of educational objectives* (2nd ed.). Thousand Oaks, CA: Corwin.

Merchant, G. (2006). A sign of the times: Looking critically at popular culture digital writing. In J. Marsh & E. Millard (Eds.), *Popular literacies, childhood, and schooling* (pp. 93-109). London: Routledge.

Richardson, W. (2006). *Blogs, wikis, podcasts, and other powerful web tools for classrooms.* Thousand Oaks, CA: Corwin.

Samuels, S.J. (1979). The method of repeated readings. *The Reading Teacher, 32,* 403-408.

Semali, L. (2001). Defining new literacies in curricular practice. *Reading Online, 5*(4). Retrieved July 15, 2008, from http://www.readingonline.org/newliteracies/semali1/index.html.

Shaughnessy, J.M., & Haladyna, T.M. (1985). Research on student attitude toward social studies. *Social Education, 49,* 692-695.

Stodolsky, S., Salk, S., & Glaessner, B. (1991). Student views about learning math and social studies. *American Educational Research Journal, 28*(1), 89-116.

Stowe, H. B. (2004). *Uncle Tom's cabin.* New York: Barnes and Noble Classics.

Weeping Time (n.d.). PBS online. Retrieved February 1 2009, from http://www.pbs.org/wgbh/aia/part4/4p2918.html.

Williams, A., & Merton, M. (2008). A review of online social networking profiles by adolescents: Implications for future research and intervention. *Adolescence, 43,* 253-74.

CHAPTER SIX

Digital Storytelling Is Not the New PowerPoint
Adolescents' Critical Constructions of Presidential Election Issues

EMILY N. SKINNER & MELANIE J. LICHTENSTEIN

Research on children's and adolescents' new literacies practices outside of school has shown that they read and utilize texts using sophisticated literacy competencies (Mackey, 2003; Vasudevan, 2006). These literacies involve engagements such as those with popular culture (Alvermann, Moon, & Hagood, 1999; Dyson, 2003); using visual and digital technologies including comics (Bitz, 2007), instant messaging (Lewis & Fabos, 2005), and fanfiction (Black, 2005); participating in online social networks (Witte, 2007); and, appropriating and transforming issues and characters presented in television and movies in writing (Skinner, 2007a).

As such, our research is situated within a new literacies perspective that posits that literacy is no longer singular and print bound; instead the iconic and digital demands of the 21st century have opened up literacies that require transversals across print and nonprint-based formats (Lankshear & Knobel, 2003). A new literacies perspective draws upon multiliteracies research that illustrates how people from diverse cultural contexts use literacy in different ways and represent meaning with multimodal texts (Cope & Kalantzis, 2000). From a new literacies perspective, text is understood as anything that can be read and comprehended or constructed to share meaning and includes reading, writing/designing, speaking, listening and viewing practices. These practices are deeply embedded within students' multiple sociocultural identities and dependent upon context (Gee, 2001).

While new literacies research has been on the forefront of literacy scholarship for the last decade in out-of-school and after-school contexts, research addressing implementation of new literacies pedagogies in classroom contexts, especially classrooms in struggling schools in high poverty contexts, is in its infancy. The dearth of research in these contexts might be explained by the recent research that that has been conducted and has illustrated the many obstacles that teachers in high poverty schools face when attempting to incorporate new literacies pedagogies into their classrooms including both instructional time constraints (e.g., pressure to focus on state test prep, district pacing calendars, competing curriculum mandates, etc.) and technology issues (e.g., unreliable computers, restrictive district filters, archaic software, etc.) (Hagood, Provost, Skinner, & Egelson, 2008).

Because of the intense obstacles that teachers have faced when implementing new literacies pedagogies in their classrooms, we believe it is especially important at this juncture also to illustrate the extensive rewards that are possible when new literacies pedagogy is presented in high-poverty classroom contexts. This chapter focuses specifically on the implementation of digital storytelling as a tool for learning about the 2008 United States presidential election issues and candidates' respective stances.

Digital Storytelling

Digital storytelling has been described as a process of connection where teachers "work with their students to help them harness the power of voice and imagery to connect people to their community by using technology that is relevant to the way we live today" (Robin, 2007, p. 429). Digital storytelling allows people to construct narrative and expository texts through combining multiple media including images (e.g., photos, graphics), voice, music, video, transitions, titles, and movement. They can then save their digital stories as movie files for playback on a computer, or they can export their stories to the internet and/or dvd.

In addition to giving students opportunities to practice new literacies, digital storytelling can be used across grade levels and content areas to address a multitude of foundational literacies, skills and strategies necessary to be successful in school such as decoding and reading comprehension of print-based texts, written composition of academic texts, and, oral fluency with Standard English grammar and vocabulary. For example, Ranker (2008) studied how two, twelve-year-old students produced digital documentaries as part of an inquiry project about the Dominican Republic. Hagood, Skinner, Venters & Yelm (2009) explored how a sixth grade social studies teacher facilitated students' construction of digital stories at the beginning of a unit of study about classic Roman civilization in order to help his students build schema around this unfamiliar content. Skinner and Hagood (2008) also presented case studies of two English language learners uses of digital stories as a context for connecting cultural identities, foundational literacies and new literacies. And, Ware (2006) examined the narrative choices and social interactions enacted by two, nine-year-old children during their participation in oral and multimodal storytelling that was part of Digital Underground Storytelling for Youth (DUSTY) literacy and technology program at Southern Methodist University.

There is a variety of digital storytelling software available, including *Movie Maker*, *iMovie*, *Voicethread*, and *Photo Story*. *Movie Maker* and *iMovie* are included with recent versions of PC and Mac basic software packages. *Photo Story* is PC compatible software that can be downloaded for free from the internet. *Voicethread.com* provides another digital storytelling context and is accessible online for free. *Voicethread* also includes a social networking element where viewers can record their comments about the digital stories in audio onto the stories.

The following case study illustrates how Melanie, an eighth grade teacher of Culturally and Linguistically Diverse (CLD) Gifted and Talented (GT) students, implemented digital storytelling using *Photo Story* as a tool for learning about the upcoming national presidential election issues. Specifically, we explored the following research questions:

1. What literacy practices did students learn from engaging in the digital storytelling projects?

2. How did Melanie's implementation of a presidential election digital storytelling unit of study position students as critical consumers and active producers of multimodal texts?

Methodology

This was a qualitative research study (Marshall & Rossman, 1999) that incorporated multiple methods of data collection including classroom observations, semi-structured interviews with Melanie and students, and a collection of artifacts from Melanie (e.g., unit handouts) and her students (e.g. completed handouts, photo stories, pre- and post-assessments). Data were analyzed using the constant comparative method of grounded theory (Glaser & Strauss, 1967) to analyze incidents from the data and to identify emergent patterns across the data (Merriam, 2001).

Melanie is a European American in her early thirties with an undergraduate degree in drama and a masters degree in drama education. She teaches sixth–eighth grade Gifted and Talented (GT) students at Laura Bailey Middle School (pseudonym). The GT students are served through a resource program that is held during each grade level exploratory class. The class curriculum is not content specific but is instead interdisciplinary and grounded in social justice teaching and multicultural education. Students meet every other day for ninety minutes. Each grade level has different themes: sixth grade curriculum focuses on elements of culture; seventh grade units concentrate on specific cultural groups and historical eras using literature, music, art, and social action; and, the eighth grade pedagogy is an intensive study in global issues and social justice culminating in students designing and implementing their own social justice action plans.

Melanie happened upon education through a theater career that led her to education outreach. Through participating in education outreach as a guest artist Melanie was able to work at schools that served at-risk and Culturally and Linguistically Diverse (CLD) students in K-12 contexts. It was with these students that Melanie found the importance of new literacies—especially for marginalized youth.

Melanie also found that drama provided the foundation to explore culturally relevant and topical material that engaged CLD students. The freedom as a guest artist allowed Melanie to focus on student interest and engagement instead of the pressure of test scores and grades. Melanie utilized pedagogical practices aimed to engage students in the cultural values and interests of the communities in which they lived. She encouraged students to make connections between their out-of-school literacies and in-school literacies while creating plays and using drama to explore issues that they found important. For example, one issue the students often endured when shopping at the local mall was racial profiling. The students and Melanie drew upon these experiences, taking on different roles from a variety of situations that the students had experienced, and then used role play to practice new skills and strategies to prepare for future encounters. Engaging in these teaching practices made Melanie's transition from being a drama teacher to a becoming a GT teacher seamless. As a GT teacher, drama and new literacies became the tools students used as opposed to products students created. The GT classroom setting emulated the freedom Melanie had found in education outreach programs.

The GT program at Laura Bailey falls under the related arts department along with Art and Physical Education. As such, Laura Bailey has one of the few remaining pullout GT programs in the district's middle schools. Ninety percent of Laura Bailey's population includes students from poverty backgrounds, and 63% of students are African American, 16% are Hispanic, 18% are White, and 3% are from other racial demographics. Of the 610 students at Laura Bailey, 82% of them receive free or reduced-priced lunch.

At the time of this study, only 5.5% of the student body at Laura Bailey qualified as GT under the criteria set forth by the state standards. Students may qualify for GT through three possible dimensions demonstrating one or more of the following: advanced reasoning abilities; high achievement in reading or math; and/or, high degree of academic or intellectual performance. Students may qualify by earning a specific score in the aptitude assessment

(93rd percentile or above), demonstrating a combination of a lower reasoning test with a high achievement score (94th percentile or above), or achieving a high achievement score and grades that average 3.75 or above on a 4.0 scale (South Carolina State Board of Education, 2004). The school principal and Melanie sought to have a greater representation of Hispanic and other underrepresented students this year. Based on Melanie's previous interactions with these students in other school contexts, they locally identified and placed students who fit the profile but may have exhibited cultural or linguistic barriers that prevented them from being identified by the state as eligible for placement in Melanie's GT class. Furthermore, they selected students who exhibited high academic performance or had shown advanced achievement in standardized tests but had not met the specific combination that the state required (Matthews, 2006).

The eighth grade GT class described in this chapter has the largest representation of CLD and locally identified students in the school. This class of 16 includes six African American students, three White students, six Hispanic students, and one Asian Pacific Islander. Seven students in the class are locally identified. In order to better serve the students and to encourage retention of underrepresented groups, Melanie designed the GT curriculum to focus on students' interests and strengths (Ford & Milner, 2005).

Classroom Implementation

Melanie's interests lie in social action and empowerment, and she has a passion for all creative modes of expression. Melanie often uses music, art, film, and drama in the classroom to explore topics of social justice. Melanie designed the eighth grade GT curriculum based on CLD GT research (Henfield, Moore & Wood, 2008; Ford, Grantham &Whiting, 2008; Ford & Thomas, 1997). Specifically, this student-centered curriculum involves four nine-week units that guide the students to: understand social justice issues, explore the ways they are expressed in arts and media, and then design and implement their own social action plan as a culminating project. For the 2008-2009 school year, the unit design was adapted to incorporate the 2008 election for the first nine weeks through exploring the political issues, teaching about the election process, and encouraging students to become more empowered to be socially active in their community.

Melanie's participation in a professional development graduate course facilitated by Emily and her colleagues at the Center for the Advancement of New Literacies in Middle Grades at the College of Charleston introduced her to *Photo Story* as a tool for digital storytelling. Emily's role as a researcher in Melanie's classroom during the digital storytelling unit was that of a participant observer. She observed and audio recorded seven of Melanie's GT digital storytelling unit classes. During the observations, Emily sat in close proximity to students and typed field notes on a laptop. On occasion during the observations, Emily interacted with students, viewing and asking questions about their projects.

There were some assumptions that Melanie made prior to beginning the project that she quickly recognized as off target. The first assumption was that the students were interested in the election. The second assumption was that the students were interested in the global issues that surrounded the election. The third assumption was that the students understood how the election and the government impacted them. These assumptions were quickly dispelled after Melanie introduced the unit on the first day of school. When Melanie told the students about the unit, they initially responded with groans, comments, and questions such as: "I don't care about politics," "Why should we have to study this, we can't even vote," and "Do we have to?" These disheartening responses informed Melanie that she needed to find a way to engage her students that was relevant to their lives. She began searching for songs that were about the election and the president to use as a catalyst for discussion. Finding songs was not difficult. What was difficult was finding songs that represented perspectives from both sides of the campaign.

Melanie decided to use *President* by Wyclef Jean (2004) as a jumping-off point to gauge where the students were in their understanding of the job of president. The song, released a month before the 2004 election, explores what Jean (2004) would do "if [he] was president." The topics Jean addresses include the War in Iraq, poverty, race issues, education, tolerance, and disease. Melanie selected this song because of the large number of issues mentioned, the popularity of the artist, and the genre it represented: Hip/Hop. *President* represents a specific point of view that provided the opportunity to explore bias in music and to explore how the artist expressed his opinions. Prior to hearing the song, students were given the writing prompt "If I were president, I would..." Many students continued to insist they did not care about politics. When Melanie asked students (all students' names are pseudonyms in this chapter) to share what they had written it became apparent that their responses did not match their protests:

> If I were president I would give document[s] to all the Hispanics, Chinese, etc. So they would be able to work (Mariana, August 25, 2008).

> I would lower gas prices by try to find and get oil cheap and easily (Brian, August 25, 2008).

Some students took more creative liberty in their response:

I'd paint the White House red and call it the 'Red House.' (Aaron, August 25, 2008).

If I were president girls would be more powerful than boys (Adriana, August 25, 2008).

During a class discussion, Melanie recorded the student ideas on the white board. Then she highlighted the broader issues under which their ideas fell. For instance, "documents" fell under immigration, "lower gas prices" related to the economy, and "painting the White House" and "more power" connected to personal freedoms and equality. This process allowed the students to see that their ideas were connected to larger issues.

Throughout the introduction of the unit it became apparent that the students needed to gain a basic understanding of the election process. Most students were not familiar with the Electoral College nor the nomination process. For example, even though at the start of the unit Senator Hilary Clinton had already conceded her bid for the Democratic nomination, most of the students were under the impression that she and Senator Barack Obama were running together. Only a few of the students had actually attended an election with their parents, and the majority of students stated that their parents did not vote. Melanie spent some time using explicit instruction to explain the election process with texts from *Cast Your Vote, Grades 6-8: National, State, and Local Government* (Vaughn, 2007). While exploring the election process, the Democratic National Convention (DNC) and Republican National Convention (RNC) occurred. Melanie instructed students to watch one or more of the keynote speakers and reflect on what they observed. She also encouraged them to watch the convention on C-SPAN to avoid the ever-present commentary found on the other networks. Unfortunately, because the conventions were on central and western time zones, the speakers were broadcast after the students normally went to sleep. To address this, Melanie set up a computer and an LCD projector in her classroom to watch the speeches found on the DNC and RNC websites.

After the students made their observations about the conventions, the class participated in Socratic seminars exploring the issues. It was at this point that Melanie observed that although the students were very "sure" of *whom* they wanted to win, they lacked background knowledge about the candidates' positions. *C-SPAN Classroom* (2008) provided supporting inquiry-based lessons to investigate the issues and the candidates' positions. To identify issues, the students used the list provided by CNNPolitics.com (2008) and selected six of the following issues to explore: abortion, economy, immigration, Iraq, education, GLBT issues, social security, guns and taxes.

Next, Melanie introduced her students to the Photo Story project. She believed digital storytelling provided the ideal multimodal design for the students to present their learning in engaging and informative ways. She assigned students to choose three issues in which they were most interested, research the background of the issues, identify both presidential candidates' positions, select quotes from both candidates that represented their positions on the issues, and articulate their own opinions with supporting evidence. The research process took a total of ten class sessions. Concurrent to gathering all of this information, Melanie and her students met in the media center which housed ten computers and worked in pairs to construct photo stories for an "undecided" voter audience.

While researching their candidates' perspectives, students engaged with multimodal texts including but not limited to: websites, editorial cartoons, popular culture songs, and images concerning the candidates. Melanie's teaching often focused on guiding students through using search engines to query and select websites and then on evaluating the validity and ideological perspectives of the websites they visited which ranged from candidates' campaign websites and news channel websites to organizational websites that were influential regarding particular campaign issues (e.g., Planned Parenthood, National Rifle Association).

Throughout the six-week digital storytelling unit, Melanie and the students dealt with complex issues and engaged in literacy practices that provided opportunities for deep literacy learning. To begin with, students sometimes found provocative images online. For example, when Mariana and Adriana, both Hispanic girls, were conducting research about the history of abortion, they came across images of aborted fetuses. Melanie did not shy away from moments such as these. Instead, she scaffolded the girls through figuring out: who published the websites, what the websites designers' perspective on the issue of abortion was, and how the website producers used images and printed text to influence their audience's views on abortion. Melanie then encouraged the girls to view websites that would have different perspectives on the issue of abortion and compare and contrast the information they engaged with so that they could present both sides of the issue in constructing their own photo stories and consider both sides of the issue when sharing their opinions.

Adriana noted that she appreciated the opportunity to think about issues they already had ideas about from their home lives while at school stating, "When we were [studying] abortion, opinions we had at home, it helped us think about them here and see. We had opinions about things already from home and we used them in Photo Story" (personal communication, October 9, 2008). Melanie considered allowing students to engage with controversial material in this context as providing them with opportunities to think deeply about their opinions. Through designating the audience of the photo stories as "undecided voters," Melanie encouraged students to look at multiple sides of issues and consider where they were situated and what positioned them there:

> I wanted to show them how they developed their own opinions... I don't think they get a lot of practice in that. They have to do persuasive letters and journaling and stuff, but how did you develop your opinion, where is that opinion coming from? What in your life made you think that? Especially the kids with the abortion stuff—they very much more aligned with McCain in that issue, but they wanted Obama to win because of how he will impact immigration and their lives. (Melanie, October 13, 2008)

In addition, students had to "translate" the political jargon so that they could understand what the candidates were talking about. Since they were going to be able to bring the project home as DVDs, Mariana suggested that they narrate in Spanish as well as English so that their parents "could see what we're doing in school" (personal communication, October 9, 2008). This created an additional challenge for the students who chose to make their Photo Story bilingual: Not only did the students have to understand the jargon in English, but they also had to translate it into Spanish. Adriana reflected on this process, noting, "It helped us whenever we were trying to say something in Spanish and we didn't know how to say it, we used a dictionary, so we looked up the words in Spanish and learned exact words in Spanish and English."

Mariana added that translating between English and Spanish was also a practice that was reminiscent of home, stating, "When we were doing it in English and Spanish, it reminds you of home, because that's how you should speak. Like, I have to translate for my mom everything in Spanish and I have to translate in English sometimes. So it mostly reminds me of my house."

In addition to decoding and interpreting political discourses and translating between English and Spanish, students also had to analyze complex images that they sometimes lacked the background knowledge to understand. As such, students' online research provided endless opportunities for Melanie to build their background knowledge and to scaffold their comprehension of complicated images. Brian, a White boy, and Aaron, an African American boy, were particularly drawn to humorous images that poked fun at the candidates and found an editorial cartoon online that satirized Sarah Palin's views on reproductive health education. In the following conversation, Melanie closely scaffolded Brian, Aaron, Sofia, a Hispanic girl, and Bree, a White girl, who were seated next to them, through decoding and comprehending a cartoon depicting a movie poster for "Juneau" starring Bristol Palin and John McCain:

MELANIE: Alright, do you know what this is about?

BRIAN: Sex Ed.

MELANIE: Did y'all see the movie *Juno*? What was that movie about?

BRIAN: It was about this girl.

SOFIA: I didn't see that.

MELANIE: Just give me a summary.

BRIAN: It was about this boy and this girl and they were friends for a long time and then like, she just popped the question about like...

MELANIE: Being intimate.

BRIAN: Yeah. It wasn't his fault. He didn't really. It's not like he just—

MELANIE: So she initiated it.

BRIAN: Yeah. She ends up with a baby and puts it up for adoption and like but she has to go through with a baby in high school. Everybody looks at her.

MELANIE: So why do you think—first of all, what is Juneau?

BRIAN: Uh, wasn't that in like uh, ...a state?

SOFIA: Illinois, Arizona,

MELANIE: It's another state that starts with an A.

BRIAN: Yeah, Alaska that's it.

MELANIE: So what does, she (pointing to Palin) have to do with Alaska?

SOFIA: She's an Alaskan.

MELANIE: And what is her job there?

SOFIA: She works there.

MELANIE: Working as? What is her job there?

SOFIA: I don't know. I've never seen that movie.

MELANIE: No, now we're talking about what's Sarah Palin's job in Alaska. She's the governor. Okay, she's the governor. And her daughter (pointing to Sarah Palin's daughter, Bristol Palin). She's the daughter of the governor and what did we find out about her?

BRIAN: She's a teenager with a baby.

MELANIE: Did she have a baby?

BRIAN: Yeah.

MELANIE: Now what does any of that have to do with this one (point to Sarah Palin)?

Brian mumbles answer.

MELANIE: What does that have to do with [Sarah] Palin and Juneau?

Brian mumbles answer.

MELANIE: But why would they be bringing up Bristol if this is about [Sarah] Palin and Juneau?

BRIAN: Because it's talking about Palin's daughter.

MELANIE: And why are people, why are people talking about that?

Brian mumbles response.

MELANIE: You mean Bristol's children? Do y'all know anything about how school curriculums are decided?

SOFIA: No.

MELANIE: So everything that y'all are taught in your academic classes are settled by standards that the state has decided and some of the curriculum things are Health, P.E., Sex Ed, things like that. The state can decide on the direction that can go, whether it means teaching abstinence only. Do you know what that means? What does that mean?

Brian's answer is inaudible.

MELANIE: Okay, or teaching about ways to have safe sex.

MELANIE: Okay, so y'all understand that there are two different approaches to teaching that—abstinence or safe sex. Alright, what would any of this have to do with Alaska?

AARON: They don't teach it in Alaska.

BRIAN: Uh, Juneau is the capital.

MELANIE: Okay, good. Who lives in the capital of the state? Now all states determine their curriculum the same way like South Carolina follows an abstinence-only policy. What do you think Alaska follows?

AARON: Sex Ed.

MELANIE: Which kind?

AARON: Abstinence.

MELANIE: Yes, and that is why they're making fun of this situation because Governor Palin insisted on an abstinence-only Sex Ed program, and people who don't support abstinence-only sex education don't think abstinence only addresses teenage pregnancy.

AARON: All of that out of that one picture! [Aaron highlights the complexity of reading political cartoons.]

MELANIE: Yep. Well, why do you think that has to do with it why?

BRIAN: Because Palin is going to be his vice president.

MELANIE: Yeah, okay. So the person who made this particular image, what do you think this is saying about McCain?

AARON: He's got his chin kind of like Popeye.

MELANIE: Okay, yeah, he does look like Popeye there, but what does this say about McCain?

SOFIA: This is an ABCD conversation.

BREE: This is an A and B conversation so C your way out of it. [Aaron and Brian were becoming frustrated with Sofia and Bree's listening in, and Bree decided to make a joke about it.]

MELANIE: So what is this saying about McCain? What specifically is this saying here? The person who made this poster—who do you think they're going to vote for?

SOFIA, AARON & BRIAN: Obama!

MELANIE: Okay, right, why?

AARON: They don't want to vote for someone who's in favor of abstinence.

MELANIE: Alright good, so when you find images like this, political humor—do you agree with that?

AARON & BRIAN: Yeah.

MELANIE: Well you can use that in your opinion section because this connects with abortion. Does that conflict with your own opinions?

AARON & BRIAN: Yeah.

MELANIE: Well y'all need to think about why do you agree with what this poster's saying and your own opinions about abortion.

Aaron's comment, "All of that in one picture," sums up the significant learning opportunities presented when students engage with new literacies texts and practices such as selecting and reading editorial cartoons in classroom contexts where teachers like Melanie are available to scaffold their learning with guided questions and elaboration on content material.

After hours of locating, decoding, comprehending and analyzing images and print-based text, translating the political jargon, searching for their own biases in their selection of images and narratives, editing their photo stories for spelling, grammar and font readability, and recording and re-recording for audibility, pacing, and tone, the students finally published their photo stories. The completed projects addressed the requirements Melanie provided in the project outline/checklist (see Table 6.1), and at the same time were flexible enough to validate the perspectives and literacy practices of the students who produced them.

Table 6.1 An Election Is Coming Unit Checklist

❑ Issue One: _____
o Explanation of the issue
o History of the issue
o At least one image illustrating the issue (*provide website where located*)
o Candidate One's position
o One quote from Candidate One about the issue
o At least one image showing the candidate (*provide website where located*)
o Candidate Two's position
o One quote from Candidate Two about the issue
o At least one image showing the candidate (*provide website where located*)
o Your opinion with supporting details

❑ Issue Two: _____
o Explanation of the issue
o History of the issue
o At least one image illustrating the issue (*provide website where located*)
o Candidate One's position
o One quote from Candidate One about the issue
o At least one image showing the candidate (*provide website where located*)
o Candidate Two's position
o One quote from Candidate Two about the issue
o At least one image showing the candidate (*provide website where located*)
o Your opinion with supporting details

❑ Issue Three: _____
o Explanation of the issue
o History of the issue
o At least one image illustrating issue (*provide website location*)
o Candidate One's position
o One quote from Candidate One about the issue
o At least one image showing the candidate (*provide website location*)
o Candidate Two's position

(Continued on next page)

(*Table 6.1 continued*)

o   One quote from Candidate Two about the issue
o   At least one image showing the candidate (*provide website location*)
o   Your opinion with supporting details

The following list includes what should be in your Photo Story:

❑   Page One
o   Title of Photo Story
o   Your name and your partner's name
o   "Laura Bailey Middle School 8ᵗʰ Grade Gifted and Talented"
o   Image that is appropriate for unit
o   If you choose to use music, please choose something that is relevant and appropriate to the project!!! (*Ms. Lichtenstein can help find songs if you cannot*)
o   Narration welcoming the viewer to your project and who you are

❑   Following Pages (at least 12 pages)
    Each issue must have at least four pages each:
o   One page for introduction to issue
o   One page for Candidate One
o   One page for Candidate Two
o   One page for your opinion or the opinions of you and your partner
o   Each page will have a narration of the information that you found
o   Each page will have text that summarizes the information

❑   Last Page
o   Credit the websites that you used
o   Identify music used including artist name and title of song

For example, Aaron and Brian's digital story (Table 6.2) was presented with a conversational tone characteristic of their favorite talk show, *The Daily Show*. In contrast, Bree and Sofia's digital story format was more similar to a mini-documentary, a genre that Bree recognized she drew from her viewing experiences both in and out of school, "It reminded me of documented movies. It reminded me of a bunch of commercials made into a movie. But, very, very, very informational commercials. Not like the type of commercials that are telling you the bad things of the others [candidates]" (personal communication, October 9, 2008).

Table 6.2 Narrative of Aaron and Brian's Photo Story

Aaron & Brian's Photo Story		
(Background music referred to by Aaron and Brian as "techno" vibe.)		
Slide Image	**Subtitle**	**Narrative**
Picture of Barack Obama	Aaron Butler	AARON: Aaron Butler
Picture of John McCain	Brian Sandusky	BRIAN: Brian Sandusky
Picture of Obama & McCain	ABMS 8th grade gifted and talented	BRIAN: Laura Bailey Middle School Eighth Grade Gifted & Talented presents:
Black and White picture of Obama & McCain	Views on political issues	AARON: Views on political issues
Picture of gun	----	AARON: Let's talk about guns, Brian. BRIAN: The issues on guns are that candidates don't want kids to get a hold of guns, illegal selling of guns and they don't want to mess with the Second Amendment.
Different picture of gun	Obama's views	BRIAN: Obama quote "that the constitution confers an individual right to bear arms, but just because you have the individual right does not mean that the state or local government can't constrain the exercise of that right."
Different picture of gun	McCain's views	BRIAN: McCain quote, "I do not believe that we should tamper with the Second Amendment."
Another picture of guns	Our views	BRIAN: I think we should stop the illegal selling of guns so that only hunters and grown adults have guns and allow guns to minors only if they have adult supervision.
Picture of warning sign at immigration border	Immigration	AARON: For many years we've had immigration, some illegal, some not. The problem with immigration at this time is that people are coming over without going through the proper legal process of becoming an immigrant.
Picture of sign to US/ Mexico	Obama's views	AARON: Obama quote: "We are a nation of laws and a nation of immigrants and those two things should be reconciled."

(Continued on next page)

(Table 6.2 continued)

Picture of child climbing fence at border	McCain's views	AARON: McCain says "I, and other colleagues, twice attempted to pass comprehensive immigrant legislation to fix our broken borders, ensure respect for the laws of this country, recognize the important economic contributions made by immigrant laborers, apprehend those who came here illegally to commit crimes."
Picture of border	US	AARON: I'm with Obama on this one because McCain wants to send people back where they came from and go through the three-year process of becoming a legal citizen, but he could be sending people's parents back and loved ones too. Obama plans to let them stay and go through the process of becoming a legal US citizen.
Boots, guns and helmets of soldiers who have been killed—Image used at anti-war events in combat photos	War in Iraq	BRIAN: The issues in Iraq are if we want soldiers out, if we will finish the war, what is needed for the war, and if we are going to go for Iraq's economics.
Picture of soldier shooting gun	Obama says	BRIAN: Obama says "The differences on Iraq in this campaign are deep. Unlike Senator John McCain, I opposed the war and I would end it as President. I believe it was a grave mistake to allow ourselves to be distracted by the fight with Al Qaeda and the Taliban by invading a country who posed no imminent threat and had nothing to do with the 9/11 attacks."
Different picture of soldier shooting gun	McCain says	BRIAN: McCain says "I know the pain war causes and I understand the frustration caused by our mistakes in this war. I admire the sacrifices made in this war by those who defend us. But I also know that a totally lost war jeopardizes our army and our nation's security. Given General Pitreas and the men and women who have given the time to succeed in Iraq, we have before us a hard road. But it was the right road and it was necessary and just."
Picture of tanks shooting	We say	BRIAN: We think McCain is leaning the right way on this issue because a lost war means economic decrease, a lost country's pride.
Picture of George Bush	Our resources: Websites listed	------

As a post-assessment, Melanie asked the students to return to their journals and reflect on the entries that they had written at the beginning of the year. Students were instructed to respond to the prompt, "If I were president..." again and reflect on how it differed from their initial entry. There were shifts in the students' engagement and connection to the issues. At the beginning of the year, Sofia wrote that she "would make everyone dress cool" (August 25, 2008). Her new entry included the issues that she had explored in her Photo Story project, "I would give Latino people an opportunity to stay in the U.S.A. I would let the GLBT people get married. Give more money to schools and teachers. I would bring the soldiers back" (October 30, 2008).

Melanie also asked the students to respond to the prompt, "If you could speak to those who are still undecided on whom to vote for what would you say to them?" T'kela, an African American girl, wrote, "I would tell them to make the choice of voting but also be knowledgeable of whom they are voting for because the candidate you vote for will change your life." (November 2, 2008). T'kela's response illustrates an understanding of how being knowledgeable about the candidates and the issues can impact the voter's choice. Bree reiterated this important idea, writing, "I would say make a pros and cons of both then go vote!" (October 30, 2008). Denzel, an African American boy, expanded further on the importance of knowing the background of the issues and being an active participant, stating, "I would tell them [undecided voters] to do research on both candidates. I would also tell them that this election will be a big part of our future. I would end my [speech by] saying 'If you want [to] be a part of something big you will vote on the 4th'" (October 30, 2008).

Discussion

Melanie's implementation of digital storytelling allowed for extensive opportunities for students' literacy learning related to a broad range of skills, processes, and practices. While students explored election issues online and designed digital stories, Melanie provided instruction on a diversity of reading, writing, viewing, speaking and listening practices including but not limited to: decoding and comprehending complex images, clarifying and determining significance of information read online, understanding and translating language presented in and constructed for different contexts (e.g., political jargon of presidential conventions versus adolescent Photo Story audience), locating and evaluating the validity of resources, determining bias, selecting information with a particular audience in mind, articulating narration so that viewers would recognize ideas as legitimate, and properly citing information. As such, digital storytelling presented opportunities for students to engage in sophisticated multimodal literacies practices reflective of the skills and practices they need to be engaged and empowered citizens in the 21ˢᵗ century.

Melanie implemented digital storytelling because she wanted to provide her students with an opportunity to use literacy for social action purposes—to educate themselves about the upcoming presidential issues through engaging in multimodal literacies and then to utilize what they learned to design digital stories that would inform undecided voters about the issues. We decided to study Melanie's implementation because we wanted to explore how digital storytelling could provide an opportunity to approach multimodal computer-based formats in new literacies ways that might position students as critical consumers and active producers of multimodal texts instead of passive recipients of content-based new literacies projects (Hagood, Provost, Skinner, & Egelson, 2008).

We found that digital storytelling offered many opportunities for Melanie to make material relevant to students and to validate their cultural identities in relation to age, gender, and ethnicity. To begin with, drawing upon adolescents' affinity for popular music, Melanie's students loved showcasing their knowledge of popular music artists as they searched for complementary music online to add to their digital stories.

Also, digital storytelling allowed for Aaron and Brian to bring their gender-based literacy practices related to humor and satire (Newkirk, 2003) to their research/design processes. Aaron further applied humor and his love for making comics (personal communication, October 9, 2008) to his understanding of the presidential candidates when he drew a manga-style comic that satirized the candidates' mudslinging campaign practices on his GT notebook (see Figure 6.1).

And, Mariana and Adriana engaged in opportunities to explore issues like abortion that were meaningful to them as adolescent girls in the context of school. In doing so, Mariana and Adriana demonstrated preferences for particular literacy practices similar to other adolescent girls (Skinner, 2007a). They further appreciated the validation of their bilingual identities and opportunities to practice translating between English and Spanish with the goal of including their parents in their school project.

The opportunity to share their digital stories with their parents as an audience was a driving motivation for many of the students. When asked about how they might use what they learned during this project outside of school, Brian responded:

> I could use this to get my ideas out or just to my family. Because kids now, they just kind of lock themselves in their bedroom and not talk to their family so they could make their Photo Story and then send it because most families have more than one

computer now, but if you have one you can just save it. Tell your mom, 'Hey go look at that Photo story I made today.' Then she would know about our ideas. (personal communication, October 9, 2008)

Aaron added:

And I could explain to my mom the different things going on, the different issues going on like right now because like my mom she doesn't pay attention to the news. She pays attention to the news as much as I do and that's not a lot so I could go home and if she's having trouble about who to vote for, I can give her some issues and tell her what's going on, what they both say about those [issues]. So it helps for undecided voters. (personal communication, October 9, 2008)

Figure 6.1 Aaron's Political Manga Drawing

In sum, all of the students interviewed explicitly recognized that they valued the opportunity to share their perspectives through narrating their digital stories. Aaron reflected:

> It kinda helps me, because I like to get my opinion out there, but me being a kid and not being able to do much with the political issues of the presidential candidates. Now I have a way to let people know how I feel without trying to fight my way to let them know how I feel. You know how people have to like strike and stuff to get heard? Well now I don't have to fight my way into it or argue with somebody. I think it helped on the Photo Story, like the part where it talked about your views, except you just type it in and the whole world gets to see it. (personal communication, October 9, 2008)

As we reflect on the multiplicity of literacy learning opportunities that digital storytelling provided when framed with the goals of creative expression and social empowerment, we think it is especially important for adolescents in high poverty contexts to have opportunities to engage with and construct their own new literacies texts so that their voices can be heard and their agency can be recognized.

Instead of continuing to marginalize students from high poverty backgrounds through imposing mandates that simplify literacy learning to application of skills to print-based texts alone, we believe that is imperative to provide opportunities for all students to engage with the range of new literacies practices that incorporate the multiliteracies of print, visual images, and media. Furthermore, students need in-school instruction that will move them beyond decoding for comprehension and into critically analyzing and responding multi-modally to print and non-print texts such as the work that other new literacies' researchers have noted (e.g., Luke & Freebody, 1997; Brass, 2008; Wilbur, 2008). This project is just one such example. We hope that future research will explore what and how additional students in high poverty contexts, not only Gifted and Talented students, but students with a range of abilities, learn when designing digital stories in classroom contexts. Moreover, we believe all students could benefit from experiences with *Photo Story* similar to Aaron who posited that digital storytelling allows adolescents to "talk about their views" and "the whole world gets to see it."

Authors' note: We would like to thank Kelly Clyborne, a College of Charleston graduate student, for the assistance she provided with data collection and organization.

References

Alvermann, D. E., Moon, J., & Hagood, M. C. (1999). *Popular culture in the classroom: Teaching and researching critical media literacy.* Newark, DE: International Reading Association and National Reading Conference.

Bitz, M. (2007). The comic book project: Literacy outside and inside the box. In J. Flood, S. Brice-Heath, & D. Lapp (Eds.), *Handbook of research on teaching literacy through the communicative and visual arts* (Vol. II) (pp. 229-237). New York: Routledge.

Black, R.W. (2005). Access and affiliation: The literacy and composition practices of English-language learners in an online fan fiction community. *Journal of Adolescent & Adult Literacy, 49,* 118-128.

Brass, J. J. (2008). Local knowledge and digital movie composing in an after-school literacy program. *Journal of Adolescent & Adult Literacy 51,* 464-473.

CNN.com. (2008). "Campaign issues." CNNpolitics.com: Election Center 2008. Retrieved November 2, 2008, from http://www.cnn.com/ELEC TION/2008/issues/

Cope, B., & Kalantzis, M. (2000). *Multiliteracies: Literacy learning and the design of social futures.* New York: Routledge.

C-SPAN. (2008). "Campaign issues." C-SPAN classroom. Retrieved November 2, 2008, from http://www.c-spanclassroom.org/campaign_issues.aspx

Democratic National Convention Committee. (2008) Democratic national convention. Retrieved November 2, 2008, from http://www.demconvention.com/

Dyson, A. H. (2003). *The brothers and sisters learn to write: Popular literacies in childhood and school cultures.* New York: Teachers College Press.

Ford, D. Y., Grantham, T. C, & Whiting, G.W. (2008). Culturally and linguistically diverse students in gifted education: Recruitment and retention issues. *Exceptional Children, 74*(3), 289-306.

Ford, D.Y. & Milner, H.R. (2005). *Teaching culturally diverse gifted students.* Waco, TX: Prufrock Press.

Ford, D.Y. & Thomas, A. (1997). *Underachievement among gifted minority students: Problems and promises.* Reston, VA: ERIC Clearinghouse on Disabilities and Gifted Education. (ERIC Document Reproduction Service No. ED409660).

Gee, J. P. (2001). Reading as situated language: A sociocognitive perspective. *Journal of Adolescent & Adult Literacy, 44,* 714-725.

Glaser, B., & Strauss, A. L. (1967). *The discovery of grounded theory: Strategies for qualitative research.* Chicago: Aldine Publishing Company.

Hagood, M.C., Provost, M., Skinner, E., & Egelson, P. (2008). Teachers' and students' literacy performance in and engagement with new literacies strategies in underperforming middle schools. *Middle Grades Research Journal 3(3)*, 57-76.

Hagood, M. C., Skinner, E., Venters, M., & Yelm, B. (2009). New literacies and assessments in middle school social studies content area instruction: Issues for classroom practices. In A. Burke and R. F. Hammett (Eds.), *Assessing new literacies: Perspectives from the classroom* (pp. 75-91).New York: Peter Lang.

Henfield, M. S., Moore, J.L, & Wood, C. (2008) Inside and outside gifted education programming: Hidden challenges for African American students. *Exceptional Children, 74*(4), 433-450.

Jean, W. (2004). President. *Welcome to Haiti-Creole 101* (iTunes Version)[CD]. New York: Koch Records.

Lankshear, C., & Knobel, M. (2003). *New literacies: Changing knowledge and classroom learning.* New York: Open University Press.

Lewis, C. & Fabos, B. (2005). Instant messaging, literacies, and social identities. *Reading Research Quarterly, 40*, 470-501.

Luke, A., & Freebody, P. (1997). Shaping the social practices of reading. In S. Muspratt, A. Luke, & P. Freebody. *Constructing critical literacies* (pp. 185-225). Cresshill, NJ: Hampton.

Mackey, M. (2003). Television and the teenage literate: Discourses of Felicity. *College English, 65*, 387-409.

Marshall, C., & Rossman, G. B. (1999). *Designing qualitative research.* Thousand Oaks, CA: Sage.

Matthews, M.S. (2006). *Working with gifted English language learners.* Waco, TX: Prufrock Press.

Merriam, S. B. (2001). *Qualitative research and case study applications in education.* San Francisco: Jossey-Bass.

Newkirk, T. (2003). *Misreading masculinity: Boys, literacy, and popular culture.* Portsmouth, NH: Heinemann.

Pink, & Mann, B. (2006). Dear Mr. President (Featuring Indigo Girls). *I'm not dead* [CD]. New York: LaFace.

Ranker, J. (2008). Making meaning on the screen: Digital video production about the Dominican Republic. *Journal of Adolescent & Adult Literacy, 51*, 410-422.

Republican National Committee. (2008). Republican national convention. Retrieved November 2, 2008, from http://www.rnc.org/

Robin, B. R. (2008). The effective uses of digital storytelling as a teaching and learning tool. In J. Flood, S. B. Heath, & D. Lapp (Eds.) *Handbook of research on teaching literacy through the communicative and visual arts* (Vol. II) (pp. 429-440). New York: Lawrence Erlbaum.

Skinner, E. N. (2007a). "Teenage Addiction": Adolescent girls drawing upon popular culture texts as mentors for writing in an after-school writing club. In E. Rowe, R. Jimenez, D. Compton, D. Dickinson, Y. Kim, K. Leander, & V. Risco (Eds.), National Reading Conference Yearbook, 55, 275-291. Chicago: National Reading Conference.

Skinner, E. N. (2007b). "Teenage Addiction": Writing workshop meets critical media literacy. Voices from the Middle, 15, 30-39.

Skinner, E. N., & Hagood, M. C. (2008). Developing literate identities with English language learners through digital storytelling. The Reading Matrix: An International Online Journal 8(2). Available: http://www.readingmatrix. com/articles/skinner_hagood/article.pdf

South Carolina State Board of Education. (2004). Gifted and Talented (Regulation Number R43-220). Columbia, SC: South Carolina Government Printing Office.

Stewart, J., & Javerbaum, D. (Producers). (2008). The Daily Show with Jon Stewart [Television series]. New York: Comedy Central.

Vasudevan, L. (2006). Looking for angels: Knowing adolescents by engaging with their multimodal literacy practices. Journal of Adolescent & Adult Literacy, 50, 52-56.

Vaughn, S. (2007). Cast your vote, grades 6–8: National, state and local government. Austin: Steck-Vaughn.

Ware, P. D. (2006). From sharing time to showtime! Valuing diverse venues for storytelling in technology-rich classrooms. Language Arts, 84(1), 45-54.

Wilbur, D. (2008). iLife: Understanding and connecting to the digital literacies of adolescents. In A. Hinchman & H. K. Sheridan-Thomas (Eds.). Best practices in adolescent literacy instruction (pp. 57-77). New York: Guilford Press.

Witte, S. (2007). "That's online writing, not boring school writing": Writing with blogs and the talkback project. Journal of Adolescent & Adult Literacy, 51(2), 92-96.

CHAPTER SEVEN

Artifactual English
Transitional Objects as a Way into English Teaching

JENNIFER ROWSELL

I think that it is very important for teachers to know what I do outside of school.

—Alicia

Not many people would take the time to take an interest in others' lives and to learn about them. Some of the things that were written in my portfolio were what I was considering doing when I graduate from high school.

—Paulette

I think that what I do outside of school should be considered in my school activities because it reflects me in a way.

—Thomas

I also appreciate how much you care about what I do outside of school. It makes me feel greatly appreciated. It's a new concept because most teachers haven't seemed this interested in what I do before. I believe that it is important to know what kids do outside of school so that you can accommodate them in the classroom also.

—Cameron

Introduction: Opening up Worlds

One humid June afternoon twenty teenagers gathered in a high school library to present portfolios of artifacts that they value and reflections about each one. For as many reasons as there were students, each one felt unmotivated in English class, yet on this June afternoon, their narratives about objects in their lives revealed a commitment to writing. Comments featured above derive from the voices of students involved in a research study in which they gathered objects that they value, often from their homes and communities, and brought them into an English classroom.

The following chapter rests on a belief that as literacy teachers, we need to open up English teaching by incorporating more vernacular texts. The reasoning behind adopting such an approach is two-fold: 1) texts today are made up of more than the written word, and we need to leverage our teaching practices on multimodal (visual, acoustic, movement) texts and practices; 2) these 'multimodal' texts absorb far more of our students' time and attention and bringing them into English teaching and learning allows for a blurring of in-school and-out-of-school boundaries. It is precisely for this reason that my central argument in the chapter relies on the notions of multimodality and Lemke's concept of (2000) 'timescale' to describe texts that absorb our time and attention.

The reality of schooling is such that there is a separation between the teaching of English and English as it exists outside of school. In "The Schooling of Literacy," Street and Street (1990) interpret a process of pedagogization whereby students are initiated into ways of being in school spaces:

> The institutionalization of a particular model of literacy operates not only through particular forms of speech and texts but in the physical and institutional space that is separated from "everyday" space for purposes of teaching and learning and that derives from wider social and ideological constructions of the social and built world. (p. 150)

Although there are objects that exist in school spaces, these objects are associated with schooling and school literacy and thereby make students who are unmotivated by English class feel disenfranchised from literacy. In addition, Street and Street (1990) acknowledge the privileging of linguistic modes in English teaching and learning over other modes of expression: "The language of the teacher and of the text positions the subject (whether student or researcher), pins them to their seats, locates them in a socially and authoritatively constructed space" (Street & Street, 1990, p. 156). There is a bracketing off of school experience from outside, lived experiences and the act of bringing in outside objects into school and writing about them blurs an inside-outside school binary. Taking up an artifactual approach to English in the research invited multimodality and cultural stories that accompany multimodal understandings of texts/objects. In this way, the artifactual opened up worlds for learners who do not quite see the point of traditional English learning prescribed by standardized curricula. *Artifactual English* as a term represents a melding together of the notions of transitional objects and 'artifacts of identity' (Holland et al., 1998).

In the research, students faced various struggles with texts. At times they felt disconnected from canonical texts; yet at other times, their struggles were associated with a dislike of essay writing. But all of the participants felt more connected to English learning when they wrote about objects from their worlds.

Crumpled Papers as Artifacts of Identity

What became a metaphor for student disengagement from English learning were crumpled-up papers in knapsacks. When students were asked to consult or to take out a particular assignment, many of them dumped out the contents of their knapsacks and flattened out crumpled bits of paper to find the desired assignment. In a sense, student participants did not recognize what it means 'to do school.' Specifically, they did not show organizational skills, comply to deadlines, or exhibit fluency in academic literacies. For example, many student participants did not understand a shift in voice, tone, and register when writing an essay for history class versus English class. The apparent lack of a socialization into what it means 'to do school' separated the participants from what they described as 'the A students.'

Nevertheless, as one of our research team noted, "their cell phones are immaculate and very organized." Holland and colleagues (1998) talk about 'artifacts of self' as valued objects that represent aspects of our identities in practice, as an index to our dispositions, interests, even histories. As artifacts of identities, their cell phones mediate their identities and choices made in the materiality of these 'artifacts of identity' and reflect interests and ruling passions. In short, students involved in our study have fluency of thought, expression, and register with their everyday objects because they have a real and valued purpose in their lives. By evoking everyday objects in the English classroom, symbolic barriers are taken down and they are able to appreciate modal shifts from one genre of object or text to another and how these objects signal different ideologies and discourse.

Artifactual English

Artifactual English is a term that signals an artifactual approach to literacy (Pahl & Rowsell, in press), as a way of approaching English teaching and learning as taking the widest possible view of texts and deconstructing how the artifactual nature of them relates to an understanding of literacy. Covering multiple genres of texts is an accepted practice in literacy teaching, but inviting texts from student worlds such as a lacrosse stick or paper cranes as carriers of meanings that relate to literacy is a fairly untraditional practice. The research study on which this chapter is based sits within a burgeoning field of literacy education that invites more informal communicational practices into literacy classrooms (Alvermann & Heron, 2001; Hull & Schultz, 2002; Knobel & Lankshear, 2007; Lewis, Enciso, & Moje, 2007; Moje, 2000; Sarroub, Pernicek, & Sweeney, 2007; Weinstein, 2006).

Students involved in the research derive a sense of self and position themselves through dress, new media objects, physical activities, digital spaces, and family/rearing artifacts. Teaching by artifacts creates a space for student voices and identities to resonate in the classroom. Artifactual English invites a "be-tween-ness" that Orellana (2007) describes as "a state of being between cul-tures" (p. 128) and artifacts offer a way of expressing a state of "betwixt and between."

Narrating Self Through Artifacts

At the beginning of the 2006/2007 academic year, I met with four high school English teachers to discuss challenges that they face as teachers of English. What each teacher agreed on was an increasing lack of interest and motivation in reading and writing by a population of students in their English class. The population of students to whom they referred takes a support English class called English Plus developed for students who scored poorly on the GEPA (Grade Eight Proficiency Assessment Test). Although students in English Plus could opt out of the project, all twenty students participated in the study dur-ing the first year, and 19 of the twenty students in the second and third year agreed to participate in the study.

Holland and her colleagues argued that identities in practice can be seen within texts. Holland and Leander (2004) similarly argued that identities be-come layered or laminated in texts and are interrelated in complex ways. Kate Pahl and I use the term 'artifact' to describe a historical aspect to the making of texts (Pahl & Rowsell, in press). Based on the work of Gunther Kress (1997) in *Before Writing*, we suggest that the materiality of texts made or valued by an individual is linked to the identity of the meaning maker and can tell us important information about the principles of their meaning making.

In this study, artifacts functioned as transitional objects. Winnicott (1971) used the term 'transitional object' to describe when a young child uses an ob-ject to create a relationship with the outside world. A blanket is an iconic tran-sitional object for an infant, representing aspects of mothering without actually taking on the role of a mother. In our study, similar principles are at work in that there is more of a relationship between student participants and their artifacts than there is between students and traditional, canonical texts.

Although there is merit in teaching classical English literature, adopting an artifactual approach in English teaching balances perspectives of historical, monomedial texts with contemporary, multimodal ones. In addition, the re-search presented in this chapter builds on work within fields such as critical literacy, which views texts as producing and reproducing culture and that texts are value laden (e.g., Muspratt, Luke, & Freebody, 1997). Such a perspective implies that our choice of text in English teaching sends out a clear message vis à vis positioning of culture, beliefs, and underlying assumptions in teaching. Elizabeth Moje (2000) in her research with marginalized adolescents found that youth invented terms and codes to develop their own language as an expression of identity. Her research illustrated how these adolescents adopted a form of apprenticeship as a way to forge identities and to create communities of practice (Lave & Wenger, 1991). Identity and communities of practice guide student interest and motivation as is clear in Moje's study and in the present one. Furthermore, this study illuminates traces of identities and ways of communicating identities materialized in adolescents' reflections and narrative writing. A key point here is that multimodalities enable individuals to express themselves in so many ways, thereby adding to a repertoire of representational resources.

From the Linguistic to the Multimodal

At the beginning of the research, English Plus had a set structure: on Mondays, Wednesdays, and Fridays students worked on vocabulary and read and wrote narratives on canonical texts such as *The Odyssey* (Fagles, 1996) or more contemporary texts such as *Black Boy* (Wright, 1966). On Tuesdays and Thursdays, students went to a space in the school called The Ideas Centre, where they received extra support from tutors on their assignments (in all subject areas). Jackie (a pseudonym for one of the teacher researchers) has a strong connection with students and with their everyday lives. Jackie and her colleagues felt that English Plus lacked a structure and life of its own. English Plus needed a core assignment or project that differentiated it from regular English class. Otherwise, the course ran the risk of being more of the same for a group of students who clearly were not inspired by their English learning. Each student showed signs of interest with print and digital texts, and, what is more, each student demonstrated that they could read and write when motivated by texts. As a result, we created what we initially called a multimodal intervention. From there, we devised written narratives about artifacts that they value, and they presented these at a year-end community event.

A Teacher-led Exploration of Artifactual English

The project took an action research, ethnographic-style (Bloome & Green, 1997) approach to collecting data. The research teams met regularly for 30 minutes to reflect on student narratives, discuss progress in the research, and make adjustments to our lessons. The meetings helped us to make revisions to our research design as we went along. For instance, we realized that students wanted more structured, detailed directions when writing narratives so we provided an artifactual focus (e.g., an object someone gave to you) and ways of discussing and analyzing the object.

Four research questions guided the study: 1) What is the relationship between valued objects and student identities? 2) How do these texts map onto English teaching content? 3) How do these texts map onto how they learn? 4) What can artifacts tell us about the principles of student meaning making? To investigate these questions, starting in January of the first year of the study, every student brought an artifact and wrote narrative reflections about the artifact based on focus questions such as, How does the artifact represent your interests (research question one)? How does the artifact reflect a relationship in your life? (research questions 1 and 4)? What do you love about your artifact (research question 3)? Questions framed their narratives and offered them a focus as they reflected on artifacts. There is a direct relationship between main research questions and focus questions for artifact reflections.

Setting

Princeton School District, well known for its university, is situated an hour outside of New York and Philadelphia and many of its residents are either commuters or academics. Princeton has a strong, long-standing African American population and relatively recent Hispanic-Latino population who live and work separately from the majority of middle to upper class residents. In the longitudinal study from which data is used for the chapter, there is a racial, cultural, and social mix in the student population.

Student participants

Over the course of the three-year study, sixty students were involved in the research. This chapter reports on the first and second years of the study with approximately 40 students. Students in the study came from Hispanic, African American, Caribbean American students, European backgrounds, and Asian backgrounds. Table 7.1 features some of the backgrounds, years of involvement, interests, and literacy struggles of seventeen focal participants (pseudonyms used). We gathered this information from surveys, and I interviewed participants in the second year of the study before they began their artifact reflections.

In our data collection, there was a goal of getting a comprehensive picture of student participants' lives, so we wanted to know not only struggles students had in English and artifacts that they value but also places and spaces that they inhabit outside of school. In this way, the study had an ethnographic approach to data collection. By 'ethnographic approach,' I am referring to a method of data collection whereby we understood the culture of the school, its community, and how these contextual understandings relate to findings. As showcased in Table 7.1, cultural backgrounds of students are diverse and although there is a pattern of disconnection with more traditional texts and interest in artifacts, each student talked about different kinds of struggles that they had with literacy.

Teacher researchers

The research team was composed of four teacher researchers in each year of the study and me. As a group, we met; we discussed and equally conceived the research design based on our students' needs and their English Plus program. All five researchers (i.e., four teacher researchers and I) are white and from middle to upper-class backgrounds; two of the teachers are relatively new to teaching with three to five years of teaching experience, and the other two teachers have twenty-plus years of experience. Framed by readings and discussions, we decided to take an action research approach and keep reflective journals on the project.

Data sources for the larger project included artifactual narratives and portfolios of each student's artifacts; digital stories (third year of the study); interviews with students; interviews with teachers; researcher reflective journals; and my observational notes.

Table 7.1 Participant Information

Student (Pseudonyms used)	Background Information (Age, Race, Culture)	Struggle with Literacy	Ethnographic/ Local Standpoint	Artifacts of Interest
1. Sienna (2nd year)	14, white, Native American and Irish	Feels like she procrastinates with assignments and has difficulty organizing herself for school	Frequents community centre for skating and developed keen interest in manga from neighbor	Drawing of female manga Warrior
2. Cameron (1st year)	14, white, American	Getting motivated to read traditional texts	Loves to watch sports, keep up on sports scores, and chats with friends online	Cell phone
3. Lara (1st year)	14, Hispanic	Sometimes lacks motivation in English class	Loves sports and doing sports in the community— from swimming to lacrosse	Lacrosse stick

Continued on next page

Continued from previous page

Student (Pseudonyms used)	Background Information (Age, Race, Culture)	Struggle with Literacy	Ethnographic/ Local Standpoint	Artifacts of Interest
4. Rob (2nd year)	14, white, Russian, Jewish	Feels "moderate" about school texts	Keen interest in news and the stock exchange. Writes stories in his spare time	A story
5. Jeremy (2nd year)	14, white, European, Jewish	Lack of interest in books for English	Avid sports player and keen on Madden football videogame; Passion for cooking	Favorite Recipe
6. Paulette (1st year)	15, African American	Struggles with school literacy because she was home-schooled until high school	Likes to play sports and hang out with friends	First teddy bear
7.Thomas (1st year)	15, white, American	Finds it hard to organize himself for English	Skateboards in the neighborhood and loves the magazine, *Transworld Skateboarding*	Skateboard
8. Taisha (2nd year)	15, African American	Does not feel connected with books studied in English class	Has a part-time job in the community and likes to text friends	Drawings
9. Iris (1st and 2nd years)	15, African American	Finds essay writing challenging	Loves Facebook	Facebook profile and teddy bear

Continued on next page

Continued from previous page

Student (Pseudonyms used)	Background Information (Age, Race, Culture)	Struggle with Literacy	Ethnographic/ Local Standpoint	Artifacts of Interest
10. Adrian (2nd Year)	14, Venezuelan and Irish	Finds it hard to get motivated to finish work in English class	Plays *Airsoft* in local parks with friends	Picture of *Airsoft* game
11. William (2nd year)	14, Caribbean American	Finds it difficult to get into English reading and writing	Listens to Kanye West, goes to Phillies games and community meetings, loves *Grand Theft Auto*	Music lyrics
12. Alicia (1st year)	15, Guatemalan	Finds it difficult to connect with literature and school writing	Writes in journal every day and listens to hip-hop and reggae	Persuasive Letter, school assignment
13. Leila (1st and 2nd years)	14, Guatemalan and Mexican	Likes writing persuasive and personal essays but does not enjoy more formal essay writing	Loves to write in her journal and to talk to her friends	Poetry
14. Maynor (2nd year)	14, Mexican	Does not have confidence in his writing	Loves to write in his journal and to write stories	Paper cranes
15. Nickolas (2nd year)	14, African American	Is not interested in traditional texts	Loves to skateboard around town with friends	Skateboard
16. Janice (1st and 2nd year)	14, African American	Struggles with reading and writing in English class and with motivation (finishing her work)	Likes Facebook and talking to friends	Cat

Analyzing Data

We opted for case studies because of the indicative, representative dimension of them. Case studies provide a picture of practice that offer compelling evidence of a *dimension* of the research. Denscombe (1998) provides a helpful insight into case study research: "the aim is to illuminate the general by looking at the particular" (p. 30). Golby (1994) has made clear that case studies are not a study of uniqueness but of particularity. Golby (1994) argues that to make understanding 'particular,' connections to other cases need to be made, and an acute awareness of how understanding is reached required. In the study, we take an 'analytic generalization' from the data to offer some insight into how we can embed a notion of artifacts and material culture into our work with adolescent learners. Invoking their worlds and their semiotic mediation of lived lives lessens a gap between vernacular and school literacies.

English Teaching as Material

The lens of practice we adopted is multimodal with an emphasis on the materiality of student work to locate deeper understandings within artifacts tied to discourses, ideologies, and modalities. By multimodal and materiality, I am signaling that students learn and are assessed on their understanding of modes that are visual, have sound, movement, and words, and these modes work in concert with each other. The argument is that English teaching is enhanced when it is materially situated because vernacular texts are predominantly composed of multiple modes, and their material qualities are fundamental to understanding them (e.g., Facebook pages with pictures and interactive games).

By looking outside of English pedagogy to the kinds of artifacts, practices, and habits of mind tied to more informal, outside literacies, it is clear that there are alternative ways of inciting creativity, innovation and motivation in English teaching and learning. Using materials (texts-photographs-objects) that students pore over, we gained a deeper appreciation of untapped literacy skills and understandings. For example, Maynor uses artifacts in his worlds like paper cranes to develop or affirm connections with friends. Yet another example is the eloquence and fluency of thought evident in Alicia's writing when she writes about something that she has experienced and is passionate about. By the end of the school year, students had not only internalized a notion of multimodality and its significance in the way that they make meaning, but also understood that this two-process of learning incites more interest and motivation.

Gunther Kress (1997) in *Before Writing* considered contemporary forms of communication as a world quite different from a '*world told* to a *world shown*"

(p. 1). As much as there are affordances to certain modes over others, there are also constraints to modes that hold texts back from their full meaning.

Artifacts and Timescales

Within the study, artifacts can be prized objects or texts produced by students, or artifacts that students value and that carry what Lemke (2000) describes as 'timescales.' Typically, participant artifacts signify identity. Frequently, artifacts produced by individuals sediment identities (Rowsell & Pahl, 2007) within texts, while in other instances, artifacts index fundamental aspects of identity. An artifact with sedimented identity is Sienna's anime warrior seen in Figure 7.1, which simultaneously depicts Sienna's love of an anime aesthetic coupled with her own belief that traditional texts blur good and bad dichotomies in characters to make them far more human-ruled by different emotions and dispositions. An artifact that indexes parts of an identity is Cameron's cell phone, which signals core parts of his identity—his best friend, his dog, his Dad.

Lemke (2000) speaks of timescales that cross over into meaning making. Timescales can be longer (tied to the past and more embedded meanings) or shorter (tied to present-day moments). He offers the samurai sword as an example of an object with a long timescale that carries a particular history. Lemke talks about analyzing literacy events on different timescales. A key finding in the study is that concentrating our gaze on what objects occupy our students' attention can help us to understand the principles of their meaning making. As Lemke (2000) notes,

> No matter how much we homogenize classroom groups—by age, by social class, by gender, by culture, race or dominant language—for the classroom processes at each timescale there will be considerable differences in affective engagement, in evaluative dispositions, in relevant knowledge and skills, and in resources for integrating the events of the moment into patterns that will persist on longer timescales. (p. 285)

It makes sense that objects and practices with which we have engaged more and longer than others carry more ideological weight in our meaning making and language activities than texts and practices confined to a school year or even a succession of years.

Finding Motivation through Artifacts

There were two unanticipated themes that arose in interview data: one is the wide-ranging nature of student texts; and the other is a keen interest in drawing and creative/leisure writing. As English teachers, it is valuable information to know that students who struggle with literacy in our classrooms are writers and representers outside of the classroom, and indeed ten participants I interviewed write and represent regularly. Take Rob and Sienna as examples. The following conversation took place between Rob and me about the texts he must read in his English class.

> Jennifer: Why didn't you like *The Lord of the Flies*?
> Rob: *The Lord of the Flies* was not very realistic or intelligent. It was violent.
> Jennifer: What about when you studied *Romeo and Juliet*, did you like it?
> Rob: Well, I guess it's a classic and you have to study it, but I don't find it too interesting.
> Jennifer: You don't? Why not?
> Rob: Because you sort of already know what's going to happen and it's really difficult to read and not an exciting story.
> Jennifer: You didn't find it exciting. Are there other Shakespeare stories that you like?
> Rob: I don't really read Shakespeare so I don't know. My parents tried to make me read *Hamlet*, but I didn't like it at all.

As adult readers we are entitled to our opinions about fiction, and Rob was articulate and specific about why he does not like *The Lord of the Flies* and *Romeo and Juliet*. The *Lord of the Flies* is violent, and we all know *Romeo and Juliet* so well at this point that we know what is going to happen. Contrast this conversation with a few minutes later when we discussed Rob's own writing:

> Jennifer: Do you like to write?
> Rob: Well, just short stories...
> Jennifer: Really? What kind of short stories do you write?
> Rob: It's like, random stuff...like whatever comes to mind.
> Jennifer: And what is the plot?
> Rob: Well, like just problems and stuff. One is about NASA.
> Jennifer: Do you want to tell me about it?
> Rob: Yeah, it was like 70 years in the future, and NASA became privatized, and it's on an asteroid, and they're trying to keep it secret because they have different chemicals that were going to be used for chemical warfare, and they didn't want any other countries to find out about it.
> Jennifer: That's really cool, Rob. Gosh, I bet you're a good writer. Would you be willing to bring that in as an artifact?
> Rob: Alright.
> Jennifer: I would really like to read it. Do you do that on your own on your own time or as part of school?
> Rob: Well, it was originally part of school but then it kind of like it wasn't because we never handed it in. It was originally supposed to be a paragraph long, but then it became a couple of pages.

Rob proceeded to say that he continues to write short stories and it has become one of his keen interests. Rob is a particularly interesting example because he shows such creativity in his fictional writing, yet he consistently maintained disenchantment with schooled literacy.

Similarly, in my interview with Sienna, she discussed her passion for manga and animé. Take Sienna's picture in Figure 7.1 as an example. Sienna struggles with literacy because she admits to procrastinating with homework due to a lack of interest. Sienna spends most of her time reading manga and animé and creating her own characters. She loves animé because "characters are not good and evil as they are in books that we study in English; they are in-between, sometimes good and sometimes bad." In Figure 7.1, you see a female warrior with ribbons that cover parts of her body. The character is mostly good, but she has a dark side that comes out sometimes. Sienna says, "I relate to animé far more because I appreciate that there are dark sides to people and that becomes a part of my stories and my pictures."

Figure 7.1 Sienna's Anime Figure

Sienna and Rob exhibit literate dispositions, an understanding of story and character development, and definitive interests in different genres of texts. Building on these funds of knowledge (Gonzales, Moll, & Amanti, 2005) would help them find a place in the English classroom.

There are ways of connecting English texts with outside texts, and there is merit in doing so. For example, exclusions from artifacts are a writerly, linguistic consciousness in their reading, writing, and representing. What seems to be missing in the English Plus student population is an implicit understanding of genre switches and linguistic tropes. Students involved in the study adopt more of a media, artifactually driven epistemology in the way that they make meaning. The act of gathering objects that they love, thinking about them, and presenting them creatively and imaginatively consolidated an understanding of how multiple modes carry affordances. You see an ontology of artifacts in Table 7.2 that features skills acquired in creating portfolios.

Table 7.2 An Ontology of Artifacts

Type of Artifact	Skills Implied
1. Artifact of Self	• Ideas are best depicted in certain modes over other modes—e.g., a photo, in some instances, says more than words can. • Artifacts express emotions. • Some materials provide more room for self-expression than others—e.g., three-dimensional objects can be held and take up important places in spaces.
2. Time-Scale Artifact	• Artifacts index memories. • Certain artifacts offer greater relevance and significance due to longevity. • Artifacts are transportable and their meaning sometimes changes in other contexts.
3. Recontextualized Artifact	• Artifacts can be recontextualized, which can change the way that we feel about them. • Artifacts can be a gateway to other learning. • Artifacts imply spaces. • Artifacts are intertextual.
4. Subversive Artifact	• Subversive artifacts give us a sense of agency. • Artifacts give us a voice that leads to other texts. • Artifacts allow us to contest ideas. • Artifacts can empower.

Materializing Identity in Artifacts: Four Case Studies of Artifactual English

Artifacts as objects of self guided the research study. Each genre of artifact reflected untapped skills and understandings of how materialities position identities in defined ways. It became clear that each artifact evoked meanings and significance to students involved in the study. There are four themes featured that arose in the data: artifacts of self; timescale artifacts; recontextualizing artifacts; and, artifacts as subversive devices.

Artifact of self: Cameron

When asked about what students were meticulous, organized, and exacting about, cell phones stood out. In their artifact reflections, some students talked about the look and the feel of their cell phones. The artifact signifies Cameron and essential parts of his character: his dog—a close friend—his Dad. Cameron claims "my phone represents who I am ..." (see Figure 7.2). The materiality of the cell phone is the first feature he talks about—it is black and shiny and has a picture of his dog in the window. Cameron's cell phone keeps him up to date on everything that is happening with his friends and family, and it bridges a gap between the local and the global (i.e., he can talk to people all over the United States). It is a key part of his enduring identity as it is lived in practice.

Figure 7.2 Artifact of Self

Artifact reflection 1 4/19/07

My artifact is my cell phone. My phone is black and it has a shiny silver trim on the outside. The outside screen has a picture of my dog on the front. I have a picture of my dog on the front because I miss her during the day. She stays home during the day. I got my cell phone at the verizon store in Hamilton. My parents bought me the phone for Christmas, so I got It on Christmas day. Actually, that's wrong I got a couple days before because the phone had to be activated. My phone means a lot to me. It means a loit because I can talk to people all over the USA. Like Desiree, she lives in PA. my phone reminds me of my dad, because my dad has the same phone. I chose my phone to represent who I am because I like my phone and it keeps me up to date with everything that is going down with my friends.

Timescale artifact: Paulette

Paulette represents timescales in her artifact reflection about a Winnie the Pooh bear that she has had ever since she was little, and the bear has been with her "through thick and thin" (see Figure 7.3). Paulette's bear signifies what Holland and Lave (2001) describe as a 'history in person.' As an object, Paulette's bear carries with it an affective behavior because of its longevity. There is a sense with the reflection on the bear that her "enduring struggles and historical subjectivities are mediated through local, situated practice"

(Holland & Lave, 2001, p. 6). Set on orange paper, there is a small picture of a bear alongside a cutout of a handsome young man above all of the cutouts sits the title, *Things dat mean da most* with a shadowing technique beneath it. The text is a meta-text of treasured objects. That is, the artifact is a collage of things that matter, which made Paulette stop and reflect on significant people and events in her life.

Figure 7.3 Timescale Artifact

He has been with me the longest... through thick and then. I first started to love him my mom and dad would get into a fight or I would be mad at something I would tell pooh, as I cried and after that I would feel so much better.

Recontextualized artifact: Lara

By 'recontextualizing artifact,' I am referring to artifacts that move a student participant from outside a context to inside a context. For example, a student not interested in ninth grade English class completes an assignment that interests and engages him. His grade reflects the investment in the content, and he then finds a place in the classroom. This shift recontextualized the student.

Lara's recontextualized artifact reflection communicates a creativity that emerges out of a new learning space—the Ideas Centre. The Ideas Centre is a space created for English Plus students to get needed support during a free period with a teacher on hand. There is the dialogic voice in "Lara's head" anticipating 'a waste of time' and in the space of practice of the Ideas Centre and the support of her English Plus teacher (another teacher involved in project), she could complete the task. The procedure of constructing a portfolio of outside and inside literacy resulted in meaning making. In this way, Lara's artifact (see Figure 7.4) recontextualizes her into a schooling space, validating her skills and knowledge of biology *in* school.

Figure7.4 Recontextualized Artifact

Artifact 4-

My fourth Artifact is my biology lab write-up. This is academically special to me because it's the first A I have gotten on a lab write up all year. Through out the year I have gotten Cs and B-s on my lab write-up's and sometimes they took too much time or I didn't understand them at all so I just didn't do them. This one was very hard for me but I just took it on and did it. Also whenever I look at it it reminds me of the first time I went to the ideas center for a tutor and used my Friday afternoon in English plus wisely and usefully. That day when we were walking down the hall to go to the ideas center I was thinking in my head the whole time that it was going to be a waste of time and all I would do was talk but then I sat down and tutor came over, helped me out and by the time the bell rang I had a full lab-write up complete and soon to be turned in for and A!

Subversive artifact: Alicia

A subversive artifact is an artifact of self that signifies a reaction to life worlds. Alicia's subversive artifact derives from an assignment that asks students to write a letter about a topic that they are passionate about. Alicia offered the artifact as an object that she values. As seen in the excerpt of the letter (see Figure 7.5), Alicia uses an impassioned voice about stereotyping and what goes along with feeling marginalized. Alicia's artifact reflects a deep sense of herself, her beliefs, and her experience that powerfully illustrate how she wants to position herself within her life world. Alicia seemed to have the most resistance to the project yet seemed one of the most enthusiastic participants during the study.

Figure 7.5 Subversive Artifact

Dear White America,

Imagine you work all day from 6 AM to late at night getting paid 8 dollars an hour, wouldn't it be unfair and also have to deal with someone telling you what to do just because you had no education? What if someone said to you, "hey, cut my grass"? It is about time for people to realize how important Hispanics are in the United States and you should stop with your stereotyping, negative comments, and mistreating other people who are not citizens.

Artifactual English: A Contemporary Pedagogy

If I return to the original research questions, many of them have been answered by this small-scale study of an artifactual approach to the teaching of English with a particular community of learners. What students value is the stuff of their lives. That is, timescale icons or a cell phone as a signifier of self. These valued objects serve as complex artifacts that conflate aspects of an identity (such as Cameron's cell phone as representative of his connection to people locally and globally) or as signifiers of aspects of self such as Alicia's letter of appeal to a reader.

What the research questions probe is an understanding of the principles of participants' meaning making. In terms of implications for English teaching, the study points to more than sparking interest in disengaged students by using texts that they like. The research points to sophisticated skills that are not as present as they could be in English teaching. For example, Sienna and Lara aptly recontextualize tacit, pleasurable literacy practices into 'schooled literacy.' Alicia demonstrates fluency of thought and expression when she writes about something that she has experienced or felt. And, Rob and Cameron's artifacts of self in their short story writing or cell phone aesthetics demonstrate their enhanced literacy skills. Objects in our study point to honed skills that are silenced in the English classroom and that once evoked, can help a student find his or her way into schooled literacy.

What seems to be missing in the English Plus student population is an implicit understanding of genre switches and linguistic tropes and more generally an academic socialization into being an 'A student'. Students involved in the study adopt more of a media, artifactually driven epistemology in the way that they make meaning. The act of gathering objects that they love, thinking about them, and presenting them creatively and imaginatively consolidated an understanding of how multiple modes carry affordances. An ontology of artifacts in Table 7.2 features skills students acquired in creating portfolios.

In light of the study, it is tougher to answer how these skills map onto English teaching and learning. For the group of teenagers involved in the study it comes down to motivation. By rendering their valued objects meaningful, students found a place in the English classroom. By validating out-of-school literacies, student participants connected more to in-school practices. By viewing a skateboard or cell phone as a text in the English classroom, students thought about voice, language, composition, process, and deeper meanings. In compiling their portfolios, participants met with me and with their teacher, related their artifacts to other texts that they study in English class, and compared portfolios with other students. Each of these concepts is quite fundamental to English teaching and learning. Rather than viewing a skateboard as an 'outside' text, allowing students to bring vernacular, valued objects and their cultural narratives into English class opens up worlds for students. Applying the project to English teaching entails more of a two-way process wherein English teachers teach canonical texts and students teach teachers about texts and artifacts that they value. If we go back to Table 7.2, allowing artifacts of identity into English teaching incites motivation; fosters critical framing of personal texts; and bridges canonical, monomedial texts with contemporary, multimodal ones. For example, Alicia's impassioned letter about racism imbued a sense of writing about an issue that really matters to her in a journalistic style. In writing the letter, Alicia understood register, style, and the function of personal narratives in writing.

Things matter. Photographs, family objects, cell phones, ipods that absorb our attention carry important information about who we are and how we make meaning. Some artifacts contest ideas and situate our perspective, whilst other artifacts foreground parts of our identity we want people to see and to recognize. The success of the project rested on reflecting on things, stuff, artifacts that matter to these students. The English classroom needs to conflate the formalism of time-honored texts with the artifactual, informal, more abbreviated texts of today. In so doing, I believe that students will find a (more) meaningful place in the English classroom.

References

Alvermann, D. E., & Heron, A. H. (2001). Literacy identity work: Playing to learn with popular media. *Journal of Adolescent & Adult Literacy, 45,* 118-122.

Bloome, D., & Green, J. (1997). Ethnography and ethnographers. In J. Flood & S. B. Heath (Eds.), *Handbook of research on teaching literacy through the communicative and visual arts* (Vol. I) (pp. 1-12). USA: Macmillan Library Reference.

Denscombe, M. (1998). *The good research guide.* Buckingham, UK: Open University Press.

Fagles, R. (Ed.). (1996). *The odyssey.* New York: Penguin Books.

Golby, M. (1994). *Case studies as educational research.* Exeter, UK: University of Exeter Press.

Gonzales, N., Moll, L., & Amanti, C. (Eds.) (2005). *Funds of knowledge: Theorizing practices in households.* Mahwah, NJ: Erlbaum.

Holland, D., & Lave, J. (2001). *History in person: Enduring struggles, contentious practice, intimate identities.* Santa Fe: School of American Research Press.

Holland, D., & Leander, K. (Eds.) (2004). Ethnographic studies of positioning and subjectivity: Narcotraffikers, Taiwanese brides, angry loggers, school troublemakers. *Ethos 32,* 127-130.

Holland, D., Lachicotte, W., Skinner, D., & Cain, C. (1998). *Identity and agency in cultural worlds.* Cambridge, MA: Harvard University Press.

Hull, G., & Schultz, K. (2002). *School's out! Bridging out-of-school literacies with classroom practice.* New York: Teachers College Press.

Knobel, M. & Lankshear, C. (2007). *A new literacies sampler.* New York: Peter Lang.

Kress, G. (1997). *Before writing: Rethinking a pathway to literacy.* London: Routledge.

Kress, G. (2003). *Literacy in a new media age.* London: Routledge.

Lave, J., & Wenger, E. (1991). *Situated Learning: Legitimate peripheral participation.* Cambridge: Cambridge University Press.

Lemke, J. L. (2000). Across the scales of time: Artifacts, activities and meanings in ecosocial systems. *Mind, culture and activity, 7*(4), 273-290.

Lewis, C., Enciso, P. & Moje, E. (2007). *Reframing sociocultural research on literacy: Identity, agency, and power.* Mahwah, NJ: Lawrence Erlbaum.

Moje, E (2000). 'To be part of the story': The literacy practices of gangsta adolescents. *Teachers College Record, 102*(3), 651-690.

Muspratt, S., Luke, A., & Freebody, P. (1997). *Constructing critical literacy: Teaching and learning textual practice.* Melbourne: Allen & Bacon.

Orellana, M.F. (2007) Moving words and worlds: Reflections from the "middle." In C. Lewis, P. Enciso, & E. B. Moje (Eds.), *Reframing sociocultural research on literacy: Identity, agency, and power* (pp.123–137). Mahwah, New Jersey: Lawrence Erlbaum Associates.

Pahl, K., & Rowsell, J. (in press). *Literacy learning through artifacts: Every object tells a story.* New York: Teachers College Press.

Rowsell, J. (2006). *Family literacy experiences.* Markham, Ontario: Pembroke Publishers.

Rowsell, J., & Pahl, K. (2007). Sedimented identities in texts: Instances of practice. *Reading Research Quarterly, 44(3)*, 388-406.

Sarroub, L., Pernicek, T., & Sweeney, T. (2007). I was bitten by a scorpion": Reading in and out of school in a refugee's life. *Journal of Adolescent & Adult Literacy, 50*, 668-679.

Street, J., & Street, B. (1990). The schooling of literacy. In D. Barton & R. Ivanic (Eds.), *Writing in the community (pp.* 143-166). London: Sage.

Weinstein, S. (2006). A love for the thing: The pleasures of rap as a literate practice. *Journal of Adolescent & Adult Literacy, 50* (4), 270-281.

Winnicott, D.W. (1971). *Playing and reality.* London: Routledge.

CHAPTER EIGHT

New Literacies and Special Education
Current Practice and Future Promise

MARY C. PROVOST & ANDREA M. BABKIE

As the first decade of the twenty-first century comes to a close, it is clear learners are being exposed to an extraordinary amount and variety of information, as well as to multiple means of creating and communicating knowledge. This change in the use and generation of information exists in the rise of the World Wide Web; in new computer tools; in the development of adaptive materials that allow access to, and production of, information; in the use of cellular telephones; as well as in new strategies for teaching. This shift in how knowledge is accessed and construed has led to a reexamination of what constitutes literacy and how literacy itself can be taught and demonstrated. A new literacies approach includes both the use of technology and the view that literacy is participatory, collaborative, and distributed (Lankshear & Knobel, 2007). Within such a framework, the focus moves to engage students via the connection of out-of-school interests to in-school learning situations, while the addition of digital technologies allows teachers to move beyond rote and/or typical learning routines through exploration of students' socio-cultural lenses and practices (Hagood, Provost, Skinner, & Egelson, 2008). Within this framework, literacies are viewed as more than reading and writing, while text includes both print and non-print media. Attention then switches to one of designing instruction that accounts for adolescents' varying engagements with multiple texts (print, audio, visual, internet, video, gaming, and so forth) and how those texts are used by students to make sense of the world (Hagood et al., 2008). For the purposes of this chapter, we approach new literacies from the perspective of focusing on students' everyday social practices (both in terms of digital use and of individual/group cultural norms). Information about those practices is then used to construct and implement intervention that allows students more flexible ways of interacting with and producing text while still demonstrating mastery of content.

For the field of Special Education, new literacies presents both a challenge and an opportunity. The challenge lies in how a new literacies approach for instruction can be meshed with the needs of learners who have difficulty with conventional print-based learning and struggle to meet mastery in a world driven by standards such as those required by *No Child Left Behind* (NCLB) (U.S. Department of Education, 2002). The opportunity lies in expanding on concepts and strategies already in place, such as Universal Design for Learning (UDL) (http://www.cast.org) to further include new technologies and a greater focus on social practices.

Professionals working with students with disabilities have historically been faced with the need to make use of technology in order for students to access and communicate information and to allow for alternative routes of demonstrating understanding and progress. Examples of this include 'talk-to-type,' Alpha Smart™, talking textbooks, and so forth. While technology use alone does not constitute 'New Literacies,' it has allowed students with special needs the opportunity to participate in socially recognized ways of negotiating content and expressing ideas, as well as to connect with individuals in their environment. Beyond the area of technology, special educators have also been faced with students for whom traditional schoolwork is a challenge, who may be alienated, at-risk, below grade level in performance of skills and/or in intellectual capability, and for whom traditional school may be seen as lacking in interest and relevance (cf. Beirne-Smith, Patton, & Kim, 2006; Bender, 2008; Lenz, Deshler, & Kissam, 2004). Thus, over the course of many years, a variety of teaching strategies have been developed and implemented with these students.

Several of these strategies adhere to the concept of a new literacies framework, specifically in terms of exploring everyday social contexts, while others could easily be adapted from their current form to be framed from a new literacies perspective. An example of the former is using comic strips when working to help students understand the social world around them and, specifically, events that have taken place in their immediate environment. By implementing an everyday form of text (comics) and using it to assist students to gain knowledge of social practices, special educators are already implementing new literacies strategies. Alternatively, an example of a current strategy that could be adapted to a new literacies model is the idea of expanding traditional teacher-made Interest Inventories (cf. http://www.kidbibs.com/learningtips/inventory.htm; http://www.orange.k12.nj.us/InclManualOrange/Inclusion Forms/STUDENTINTERESTINVENTORY-OrangeInclusionManual.pdf) to ones in which the teacher gains knowledge of, and is able to connect instruction to, out-of-school and in-school literacies so as to garner students' attention and build on their motivation of successes with out-of-school texts to frame and to make relevant in-school texts.

Students with mild disabilities experience a number of difficulties that create problems with accessing and using traditional text resources, as well as with creating text itself. These difficulties range from deficits in print-based reading and written language skills, to issues with determining the relevance of classroom materials, to problems in all aspects of analyzing text. Additionally, many students lack receptive and expressive interpersonal communication skills, either due to an inability to read cues derived from body language and facial expression and/or difficulty understanding specific language usage such as sarcasm (e.g.,http://www.autism-society.org/site/DocServer/NEWasagrowingup-teen-final-rev.pdf?docID=11041).

The purpose of this chapter is to discuss the difficulties shown by students with mild disabilities at the middle and secondary levels in terms of accessing and communicating information; to describe research regarding teaching strategies, technology, and materials currently in use with these populations; to investigate commonalities between current practices and those from a new literacies framework, and to explore the untapped potential new literacies offers these students.

Overview of Learners with Mild Disabilities

The area of special education focusing on students with what are considered mild disabilities is anything but homogeneous. Students within this classification may be identified with Learning Disabilities (LD), Attention Deficit Hyperactivity Disorders (ADHD), Emotional/Behavioral Disorders (E/BD), Autism Spectrum Disorders (ASD), or Mild Cognitive/Intellectual Disabilities (MR/ID). Thus, learners with mild disabilities may demonstrate wide and varied differences in how information is received and processed, as well as how it is communicated to others. For the purposes of this chapter, only a brief overview of common characteristics with regard to processing, communicating, and organizing information, as well as social skills development, is detailed. (For more in-depth information on these areas, please refer to suggested texts listed after the references.)

Students identified with Learning Disabilities (LD) are a particularly heterogeneous population, with a variety of issues in terms of just how the disorder is defined (Hardman, Drew, & Egan, 2005). Defining characteristics of this population include difficulties with information processing, or how information is acquired, retained, and manipulated (Gettinger & Seibert, 2002), including memory processes and organization; executive function (planning, organizing and self-regulating/self-monitoring skills [Meltzer, 2007]); metacognition (Flavell, 1979); strategic problem solving (Fuchs, Fuchs, Hamlett, & Appleton, 2002); and difficulties with attention or focus on task (Bender,

2008), including understanding relevant dimensions of material presented. The last characteristic is one also demonstrated in students with Attention Deficit Hyperactivity Disorder (ADHD), leading to frequent comorbidity or overlap within the groups (Forness & Kavale, 2001). It is important to note, however, that not all students with LD exhibit hyperactivity, nor do all students with ADHD exhibit LD.

The diagnosis of ADHD (Attention Deficit Hyperactivity Disorder) is not a separate category of special education but nonetheless accounts for over 40 percent of all students in programs for Emotional/Behavior Disorders (E/BD) and about a fourth of all students in programs for LD (Forness & Kavale, 2001). Students with ADHD often have significant difficulties in school both in terms of impulsivity and other behavioral issues, as well as with academics, with deficits apparent in executive function, and/or the ability to monitor and regulate behavior (Rucklidge & Tannock, 2002), as well as with selective attention, or the inability to focus on the central task or information (Faraone, Beiderman, Monuteaux, Doyle, & Seidman, 2001). In the past, this group of students was divided into two subgroups: ADHD and Attention Deficit Disorder (ADD) with the difference being that students with ADD did not demonstrate hyperactivity but did demonstrate deficits in selective attention. In recent years, ADD has been subsumed under the ADHD umbrella, with the defining characteristic being that of attentional deficits. For many students with LD and those with ADHD, social-emotional and interpersonal difficulties are also apparent, with low self-esteem and misunderstanding of social cues (Cosden, Brown, & Elliot, 2002; Vaughn, Erlbaum, & Boardman, 2001). This overlap of difficulties in social skills and emotional control has at times made it difficult to differentiate students with LD or ADHD with students identified as having Emotional/Behavioral Disorders (E/BD).

Students with E/BD also can be considered a heterogeneous group, with subcategories including conduct disorders, anxiety-withdrawal disorder, and oppositional defiant disorder among others (Hardman et al., 2005). As with students with LD, students with E/BD tend to have average intelligence (Algozzine & White, 2002) but frequently demonstrate an inability to learn that cannot be attributed to known factors (U.S. Department of Education, 2004). Students with E/BD often experience significant difficulties in academic subject areas (Algozzine & White, 2002), with drop-out rates that are considerable (approximately 52% of these students leave school prior to 10th grade [U.S. Department of Education, 2002]). The deciding factor for E/BD is generally the length and severity of the social, behavioral, and emotional difficulties in comparison to typical students (U.S. Department of Education, 2004).

Students with Autism Spectrum Disorder (ASD) may demonstrate some of the same needs as students with LD or E/BD, chiefly with regard to difficulties with metacognition, executive function, and social skills development (Russell, 1997; Winner, 2008). A high percentage of these students also have signs of ADHD (Attwood, 2008). As the focus of this chapter is on mild disabilities, rather than looking at all students on the spectrum, our discussion concerns those students identified with High Functioning Autism (HFA) and Asperger Syndrome. While there is disagreement as to how or even whether to differentiate these two subgroups, students with Asperger Syndrome tend to have typically developing language and cognitive skills and are often not diagnosed until they begin school (Attwood, 2008), while those with HFA show early signs of delay, particularly in the area of communication. As ASD is a spectrum disorder, students so identified may fall anywhere along the continuum from significantly delayed to fairly typical in communication, cognition, and social dimensions, thus also representing a population that is extremely heterogeneous. That said, there are common characteristics that may occur with varying levels of severity (Boutout, 2006). These include (but are not limited to): resistance to change and insistence on sameness; sensory sensitivity; preference for being alone; repetitive behaviors; difficulty with initiating or sustaining conversation; and difficulty with understanding social cues.

The last group to be discussed within this section addresses students with mild cognitive/intellectual disabilities (MR/ID). Unlike the groups discussed previously, students with this classification do show significant deficits in cognitive and adaptive behavior. Students demonstrate difficulties with reasoning, planning, abstract thinking, learning from experience, communication, skills for functioning in everyday life/life skills, and social understanding (Beirne-Smith et al., 2006). Even students with mild levels of intellectual impairment may have difficulty living independently in adult life. As a result, the educational interventions often focus on developing skills (academic, social, and functional) that will lead to the greatest independence as adults.

For each of these groups, special educators have, of necessity, designed and implemented strategies to address unique needs in areas such as metacognition, attention, organization, determining relevance, learner engagement, and social understanding. Additionally, management of behaviors has frequently been a priority for intervention, as has the use of technology in order to assist students in accessing and communicating information.

Technology and Special Education

In many ways, the field of special education has been in the forefront in seeking ways to engage students and to provide alternative routes to connect with others, access curriculum, and demonstrate literacy and learning. This is particularly true in the area of communication, where some of the earliest uses of technology and its integration into the classroom come from the field of special education and assistive technology (Edyburn, 2003). Student inability to access information and communicate knowledge has been an issue for many years, whether in terms of deficits in spoken and/or written language, in the skills to control motor movements to write or type, or in the ability to organize and communicate ideas. As a result, a number of different adaptive and alternative means of communication have been developed, whether for using technology, gaining information, sharing information in spoken or written form, or interacting with others in the environment. Materials available for students range from expanded keyboards, word prediction programs, talk-to-type software, scanners for texts, Picture-It™ software, Board-Maker™, Write Out-Loud™, and a multitude of other products (see for example, Don Johnston Products: http://www.donjohnston.com). Kurzweil Education Systems (http://www.kurzweiledu.com) provides scaffolded reading, writing, and study skills solutions, allowing educators to provide differentiated instruction without having to differentiate the curriculum, while the Accessible Book Collection (http://www.accessiblebookcollection.org) offers educators digital texts for use with learners. Microsoft Word™ provides many options to make reading and writing more readily available; and sites such as the National Center to Improve Practice in Special Education through Technology, Media, and Materials (NCIP) (http://www2.edc.org/NCIP), the National Center for Supportive E Texts (NCSeT) (http://ncset.uoregon.edu/), and the Center for Applied Special Technology (CAST) (http://www.cast.org) provide information on technology and special education. For students requiring assistance in organizing their thoughts for writing, Inspiration Software™ (http://www.inspiration.com) has and continues to be a leader in the field, providing graphic organizers for brainstorming, organizing, and analyzing material. KidSpiration™, an off-shoot of Inspiration™ Software, was developed to allow students to design their own organizers. Materials have also been developed to assist students with ASD learn verbal and facial social cues through interactive multimedia (Golan & Baron-Cohen, 2008). The products and sites noted above represent but a small portion of the available materials designed originally for students with special needs that are now in some instances used throughout the educational community.

While the use of technology is not the sole component of new literacies, the very fact that many individuals with mild disabilities have historically required alternate means to allow engagement and communication has helped to create an environment in which these students can participate in social practices and socially recognized ways of using language, thus permitting connections with others. If literacy is to be participatory, collaborative, and distributed (Lankshear & Knobel, 2007), it first must be something that can be analyzed and produced. The challenge for educators working with students with mild disabilities, and who are interested in implementing instruction using a new literacies approach, now involves taking the next steps and using technology not only as a tool for access but also in designing instruction that allows a connection based on socio-cultural perspectives and out-of-school technology usage, leading to increased engagement and relevance for students. This can be done through learning about and implementing new literacies strategies and using them in combination with teaching strategies currently in use in special education classrooms.

Teaching Strategies in Special Education

While teaching strategies of necessity vary widely based on the specific and unique needs of the different subgroups of students identified with mild disabilities, some things are constants. Among these is the need to involve and engage learners through making use of materials that are relevant to student interests and knowledge. Materials such as high interest-low readability books and materials have been used for decades (e.g., see publisher Steck-Vaughn's *Lynx Graphic Novels* for grades 6-8 with grade 3 reading level), as have teen magazines and newspapers. Using technology to allow access and communication has been part of the teaching process for a number of years. For students with organization difficulties and who may have trouble in determining what is relevant in texts and lectures, as well as making sense of concepts, tools such as graphic organizers and content enhancement strategies have been developed (e.g., Ellis, 2004), as have a variety of metacognitive strategies to assist students in learning about how they think, leading to understanding and producing content (e.g., Kansas Strategies Strategic Instruction Model [SIM™]: http://www.kucrl.org/). Cognitive behavioral interventions for fostering social competence have been used with students to explore their own behavior through metacognition and are designed to assist student in understanding and monitoring problem situations (Simpson, 2005). While the above represent but a small slice of the techniques, strategies, and methods used by special educators, they are indicative of the many and varied approaches that have been developed and implemented over the years. These instructional aides draw on the multiliteracies of students' lives, connecting various texts in an effort to ensure students with mild disabilities have the opportunity to develop the literacy and communication skills needed in adult life.

Special Education and New Literacies: Reworking and Expanding Current Strategies

While, if one were to couple the terms 'Special Education' and new literacies into a search engine, little or nothing would come up, the special education research community has done much in exploring today's students' technology usage and its subsequent impact on students with disabilities (see, for example, the work done at the University of Oregon's NCSeT project: http://ncset.uoregon.edu/). Additionally, CAST's work has, for almost two decades, focused on Universal Design for Learning (UDL) and the need for *Multiple means of representation,* designed to provide learners various ways of acquiring information and knowledge; *Multiple means of action and expression,* intended to allow for and to promote learners having options in demonstrating what they know; and *Multiple means of engagement,* to draw on learners' interests, offer appropriate challenges, and increase motivation (http://www.cast. org). Over the past several years, with research projects such as The Composition Initiative, CAST worked to examine ways in which digital technologies can help students communicate what they have learned while developing the pedagogies and techniques to make those technologies most effective in the classroom. Thus, while not necessarily recognized in the new literacies literature, some of the techniques used in special education programs bear a resemblance to those used in these authors' approach to new literacies, both in terms of students' everyday social practices of digital use and of teachers using that knowledge to construct and implement intervention that allows students more flexible ways of interacting with and producing text while still demonstrating mastery of content.

In the area of special education, creating comic strips has existed for some time as an intervention tool to explain social issues to students with Autism Spectrum Disorder (ASD). Introduced by Carol Gray in 1994 to teach students social skills and to improve social understanding through explaining the 'whys' and 'whats' of various situations, comic strips have also been used as a positive behavioral support strategy for students (Glaeser, Pierson & Fritschmann, 2003). An additional component of comic strips is 'Social Stories™', which are generated by students with higher verbal and written language skills. Social Stories™ are designed to assist students in evaluating social situations to which they need to respond or to which they have demonstrated inappropriate responses. Students use a brief narrative to describe the situation, identify relevant social cues, and indicate possible/ appropriate responses (Rogers & Myles, 2001). A modified version of comic strips that incorporates elements of social stories and is used with students with more limited communication skills is 'Comic Strip Conversations'™. Comic Strip Conversations and Social

Stories, through engaging the student in processing the environmental information with which they must cope, have proven successful in helping students with ASD comprehend the social world around them.

By using an expanded view of text (comics) and situating them as tools to help students navigate the social world, this strategy used in special education certainly falls within a new literacies framework. For students with LD, ADHD, E/BD, and MR/ID, comic strip writing could be expanded to encompass the *Comic Writing* that has been investigated and implemented by researchers and teachers involved with new literacies (*Curriculum Review*, 2004). Based on the concept of participatory literacy, the Comic Book Project "puts children in the role of creators, rather than merely receivers of information. Children write and draw about their personal experiences and interests, thereby engaging them in the learning process and motivating them to succeed in school, after school, and in life" (http://comicbookproject.org/index.html? gclid=CPCB5t7NwJYCFQITswodoGY_xw). Building on Bitz's work from the Comic Book Project (2004), faculty members and teachers involved in the Center of Excellence for the Advancement of New Literacies in Middle Grades grant explored the creation of comic books in English language arts and social studies classrooms (Hagood et al., 2008). Teachers attended an invited session conducted by Bitz, in which information was presented on his project and teachers were able to view student produced products. Teachers involved in the work of the grant embraced comic books as a genre for writing during the school day, finding not only that writing and illustrating comic books served to engage students in learning, but also that use of this genre allowed for students to make personal connections with text and content. This participation and collaboration in writing comic books allowed students to demonstrate comprehension of multiple texts in a distributed fashion, increasing engagement and understanding of content material.

Using visual texts for reading comprehension can provide another opportunity for special educators to implement an expanded version of text that is socially relevant into their teaching. An example of such visual texts is *Manga* (Japanese comic books), which have become very popular with children and adolescents in the United States (Schwartz & Rubinstein-Avila, 2006). The efficacy of using of this popular culture medium in literacy instruction for adolescents appears to be based on the multimodal and semiotic writing styles. Additionally, engagement with others with the same interests creates opportunities for shared experiences (Alvermann & Heron, 2001) and the potential for social skills development.

Think-Aloud protocols are used in special education as a means to evaluate reading comprehension from the perspective of assessing strategic learning behaviors (Myers & Lytle, 1986). Essentially, a Think-Aloud procedure is designed to assess reading comprehension by asking the student to think out loud while reading the passage and responding to questions, thus allowing the listener to determine processes used in making inferences and strategies used to facilitate comprehension. Laing and Kamhi (2002) examined the use of think-aloud protocols as a tool for comparing inferences made by students with average and below average print-based reading abilities. Student comments were analyzed for rate and kinds of inferences made while reading. Inferences were classified into three basic types: predictive (speculates about events or actions that may occur based on what has already occurred in the story), associative (a statement that makes generalizations about characters, actions, objects, or events in the story) and explanation (causal connections between actions and events in the story that are usually responses to *why* questions providing responses for a state, event, or action). To develop this technique into one that makes use of an everyday socio-cultural context using an expanded definition of text, movie trailers could replace traditional text as an aid for comprehending visual texts, critical thinking, and predicting and inferencing, a process being implemented in new literacies research.

Using the movie trailer for the film *The Pursuit of Happyness* (Columbia Pictures, 2006), Skinner (2007) modeled for teachers working with the Center of Excellence for the Advancement of New Literacies in Middle Grades how using movie trailers could be an alternate medium for developing comprehension of text. Skinner demonstrated to teachers various instructional techniques using specific portions of the trailers, using classroom students as participants and teachers as observers. This allowed teachers to examine the implementation process, as well as to appreciate the benefit of the medium through witnessing students' engagement and responses. A specific example was watching the part of the trailer in which the lead character sleeps with his son in a public restroom. His foot was propped against the door to prevent others' entry, tears trickled down his face and his son slept in his lap. Students were asked questions as to why they thought he was sleeping in a public restroom, how he might be feeling, why he had his foot propped against the door, and so forth, in working to help them use visual images to draw inferences about the character, the setting, and the situation in which he found himself and his son. Using such a familiar medium to teach critical thinking skills not only may serve to engage students but also demonstrates to them the need for the instructional content being taught.

Interest Inventories (Elksnin & Elksnin, 1993) have been used in special education to gain information about students for planning relevant and timely instruction. Typically the teacher designs a questionnaire asking students about likes and dislikes, hobbies, interests, and so forth, as a strategy to obtain personal student-centered information as a basis for designing relevant and engaging instruction focused on print-based literacy development. An expanded, new literacies version of an interest inventory that captures socio-cultural and digital use information is the *Popular Culture Survey* (Hagood, 2007). Teachers use a written template to compare their personal literacies to those of their students and then analyze the similarities and differences between the literacies these two groups use. The survey captures information on an array of texts, including television shows, movies, music, books (best sellers, series books, graphic novels, etc.), magazines and comic strips, websites, video games, fashion, and other (e.g., trading cards, hobbies, sports, etc.). After teachers and students complete the survey, they reflect on the following questions: a) What makes these texts/practices popular for each group?; b) Thoughts about similarities and differences between teachers and students; and c) How do popular culture texts represent your identities (e.g., teacher, mother, American, friend, White 30-something-year-old woman, surfer, gardener, guitarist)? By using the survey, teachers gain knowledge not only of their own literacies but also that of their students. This information can then be incorporated in developing projects and instruction that should better engage students as it is based on their interests and socio-cultural perspectives.

Another new literacies approach which assists teachers and students in exploring their new literacies practices is the *Literacy Practices Ethnography* (Skinner, 2006), whereby students investigate the role of new literacies in their lives and think about how their purposes for using new literacies represent their multiple identities. The ethnography template requires teachers and/or students to initially list a text, to then list when, where, and with whom did they engage with the text, and finally, to document the purpose for engaging with the text. For example, students might say that they watched the television show "Pimp my Ride." They watched the show in the afternoon by themselves while talking on the telephone with a friend. The purpose for watching the show was entertainment and to get ideas for pimping own vehicle, while speaking on the phone allowed for a shared frame of reference. The ethnography serves as a diary of literacy practices. This information can then be translated by teacher and student into ways of analyzing preferred learning activities, as well as social interaction processes, which can later be used in guiding selection of materials and means of designing instruction.

Repeated Reading has been a fixture of special education for many years, with extensive research conducted with respect to fluency rates for students with and without disabilities (O'Connor, White & Swanson, 2007; Rasinski, 2004; Therrien & Hughes, 2008; Vadasy & Sanders, 2008). For example, O'Connor, White and Swanson (2007) studied the impact of repeated reading versus continuous reading procedures on the reading fluency and comprehension of students with and without disabilities. Results showed students in the treatment group had significant differences in fluency and comprehension performance in comparison to students in the control group. The importance of repeated readings as a way of increasing fluency in use of decoding skills has also been studied (Rasinski, 2004). Therrien and Hughes (2008) investigated the relationship between repeated reading and question-generation on students' reading comprehension and fluency for students with learning disabilities and/or at-risk for reading problems. They found that repeated reading improved fluency rates on reread passages and was more effective than question-generation in increasing student factual comprehension of material.

In a new literacies application of repeated readings, making use of the socio-cultural background of students, Hagood and Ash (1999) investigated *The Karaoke Strategy* as a reinforcement tool for increasing student reading fluency. Initially, they conducted a music survey with students. This survey asked students to a) name three of their favorite songs; b) tell why they liked each song; and c) to describe what the lyrics of each song meant. After completing these steps, each student self-selected a song from one of his/her favorites. Then students retrieved the lyrics of their favorite songs from an online source and printed them for repeated readings. Next, each student participated in a peer-monitored repeated reading session of selected word passages with the goal of making fewer than two errors per reading. When students accomplished this goal, they completed a karaoke performance of the self-selected song. The lesson/strategy concluded with a group discussion of the various song lyrics. Hagood and Ash's results demonstrated that using karaoke was effective as a motivator for students decoding printed text read aloud with accuracy.

Technology in New Literacies and Special Education

Technology is a significant component of new literacies and in special education. In a new literacies framework, integrating technology into the classroom plays a major role in connecting student out-of-school interests with in-school instructional activities and is in itself seen as a form of literacy. With the central idea of understanding, meaning, and context, digital literacies are, as noted by Bawden (2008), an "essential requirement for life in a digital age" (p. 30). In a new literacies framework, 'digital literacies' clearly delineate between the process of mastering the technical skills of technology usage and the cognitive and social-emotional aspects of working in a digital environment (Lankshear & Knobel, 2008). As noted by Lankshear and Knobel (2006), the purpose of using technology in the classroom is not merely to replace written essays with PowerPoints, or as the authors put it "old wine in new bottles" (p.55), but, rather, the focus is on constructing new knowledge, creating media expressions, and communicating with others (Martin, 2005). Digital literacies assume a significant role in the tenant of shared and distributed content as an important component of new literacies. As noted by Robin (2008), integrating technology in the classroom goes beyond merely adding computers and software. This view is also held by those in the forefront of digital literacies research, who believe the focus should be on ways in which technology can be used by teachers to change the dynamic of instruction and by students to manipulate and share information (Riesland, 2005). *Digital Storytelling* is an example of digital literacies that offers enormous promise within a new literacies framework. In a review of the development and use of digital storytelling, Robin (2008) discusses the ways in which the technique can be used, including multimedia-rich teacher-created stories used as a hook to capture student interest; students creating and sharing their stories as a way of increasing engagement; and capturing student attention by meaningfully integrating emerging technologies into the classroom.

Technology requirements have been a part of special education law (U.S. Department of Education, 2004) for decades. In 1998, Congress amended the Rehabilitation Act to require federal agencies to make their electronic and information technology accessible to people with disabilities (Section 508 [29 U.S.C. '794d]). In the same year, the Assistive Technology Act of 1998, (105-394, S.2432) was also passed. As noted previously in the chapter, numerous websites and journals (e.g., *Journal of Technology and Media*) exist to inform special educators of ways to access and use the web to assist in student learning. Some examples of the research in this area include: using the web to increase creativity and enhance process writing (Smith, Boone, & Higgins, 1998); using multimedia inquiry projects in order to master content in inclusive general education classrooms, with the additional result of increased motivation, engagement and application of reading comprehension strategies (Elder-Hinshaw, Manset-Williamson, Nelson & Dunn, 2006); the use of WebQuests and ways in which to modify their use through strategies such as graphic organizers, hypertext study guides, and creating templates for compiling information (Skyler, Higgins, & Boone, 2007); and using technology in the form of hypermedia, online research, PowerPoint, and word processing with a group of at-risk middle school students in which findings suggested accepting ownership of work and using a variety of technology methods to demonstrate knowledge led to gains in reading and writing skills (Little, 2006). Additionally, special educators have explored the implementation of digital stories as a means for increasing social skills for students with disabilities (More, 2008). Digital media have also been found to increase student engagement and learning by using familiar individuals and environments (Moreno, Mayer, Spires, & Lester, 2001).

Components of digital literacies that could be implemented in special education classrooms to encourage students to communicate ideas based on their own social constructs in a non-threatening manner include using *blogging* on topics of interest; accessing and participating in online sites such as Fan Fiction (http://www.fanfiction.net/) for both producing communication and reviewing others' work; using *texting* as a means to engage students in the writing process; and participating in wikis to analyze and provide content. These literacies have been used and researched with students in the regular education classrooms. For example, Thomas (2007), in her chapter reviewing the use of Fan Fiction, discusses the impact participation in such sites has not only on narrative skills and collaborative construction of narrative worlds, but, equally importantly, on a sense of identity and the development of friendships. Ito (2008), in speaking on the Digital Youth Project, discusses the use of blogging and texting as avenues by which students are creating and sharing their digital works in a context of public scrutiny. As she notes, "for a majority of youth now in the US, tools for writing, creating and modifying digital photos and videos, and communicating on the internet are part of their everyday life. The unique affordances of digital media—to make, remake, modify, mashup, and remix media content are taken for granted now (2008, no page)." By using blogging, sites for writing and reviewing others' work, and participating in the development of information for the internet, students engage with literacies in socially recognized ways of using language that identify them as part of a group and offer the educator opportunities to develop students' skills while providing necessary content.

From the perspective of developing and improving social skills, video gaming is a common form of entertainment and socialization. Using the concept of playing to learn (Alvermann & Heron, 2001), there is potential to design interventions in which online multiplayer gaming with headset connections for communication might be used to facilitate the development of social skills and of working together as a group to gain an objective (such as winning a victory). Additionally, students could practice problem-solving and strategizing in achieving their goal. The use of *virtual realities* such as Second Life™ offer students opportunities to practice social engagement in an environment in which the need to read facial and gestural cues is removed. *My Space* and *Face Book* present multiple avenues for social engagement, while sites such as *YouTube* provide students the chance to share their work and experiences. A number of researchers are examining the potential influence of digital literacies on social development and networks, including the concept of identities, using technology to extend social worlds, and connecting to peers who share similar interests (cf. Ito et al., 2008). Ito et al. (2008), in reviewing the findings of their three-year research study of youth media use, discuss the increasing prevalence of different digital media in the lives of youths and young adults in the U.S. today. How these students navigate their social worlds; extend existing and form new friendships; and engage in self-expression by selecting what they want to portray about themselves in the design and content of their personal web pages all attest to the increasing importance and participatory nature of digital literacies. Educators need to be familiar with, and explore ways in which to integrate into the classroom, the social aspects of new literacies as another avenue by which students, particularly those for whom social interactions may be a challenge, can create and navigate new forms of self-expression.

In reviewing the use of various intervention strategies that are analogous in both special education and in new literacies, it is apparent they share similar goals in terms of engaging students, creating student interest, and in making connections both with students and in students' understanding of material. These goals serve as a significant aspect of how instruction is constructed and delivered. Ultimately, the focus, regardless of educator background or theoretical leanings, is on the development of student skills and knowledge. What new literacies offers special education is another lens through which to view literacy and a new means for developing interventions with students, particularly in terms of connecting in-school and out-of-school interests and technology, thus leading to instruction that is more engaging and relevant to learners.

Each of the strategies discussed above has the possibility to offer enormous potential to special educators working with students with mild disabilities. Learning more about interest in different texts and why those texts are important can assist teachers in designing more meaningful activities for learning and helping students connect and develop their literacies across text forms. For learners who struggle with traditional academics and question the relevance of what they are learning and how it is taught, a new literacies framework gives teachers a new and different approach. Using relevant and high interest materials in an instructional design viewed through a socio-cultural lens, coupled with a multidimensional approach, allows professionals to design classroom instruction that has potential to increase students' investment in learning. Should such an investment occur, growth not only in terms of cognitive understanding but in the social skills gleaned through the shared experiences involved in participation and collaboration may easily follow.

Example of Research Using New Literacies with Students with Mild Disabilities

In the winter of 2008, Jill Brown, a special education teacher participating in the Center of Excellence for the Advancement of New Literacies in Middle

Grades grant, housed at the College of Charleston, implemented a four-week new literacies project with a group of middle school students. The school was, and is, considered low-performing as a result of test scores on Measures of Academic Progress (MAP), quarterly assessments given to students in reading and math, and on year-end state assessments of the Palmetto Achievement Challenge Test (PACT). Students attending this school were/are largely from low-income African American households. The students who participated in this particular new literacies project received services in a self-contained model, grades six through eight, of instruction for students with emotional and learning disabilities. The majority of the students were African American and performing significantly below grade level.

The new literacies unit entitled, "Jump the Broom," signaled a new beginning for these students as part of a broader topic of "Black History Month." Students orally interviewed family members (taking written notes and/or audio-recording the interview, when possible), seeking information about the students' early childhood, wrote a brief autobiographical piece reflecting the students' life at present, and then wrote a prediction of their lives in the future. Students also compared their lives to African American figures (e.g., Joe Louis, Carter G. Woodson, and Elizabeth "Bessie" Coleman), living or dead. They researched each figure using the internet (Wikipedia, Google, Yahoo, etc.) and/or books and other educational resources and created tri-fold brochures, with graphics, depicting each. Students created PowerPoint presentations summarizing their work and then performed and/or read from their work. The "Jump the Broom" activity culminated with a traditional southern meal and actual jumping of a broom to signify a new beginning for students as was customary in the time of American slavery (http://www.urbandictionary.com/define.php?term=jump%20the%20 broom). During the unit, Ms. Brown reported that her students were highly engaged and that there was an increase in student attendance at school. Furthermore, students who typically did not participate in class completed the project.

This project offers an excellent example of a new literacies ethos of participatory, collaborative, and distributed learning, by focusing on using relevant and high interest materials in an instructional design viewed through a socio-cultural lens paired with technology. Through the "Jump the Broom" project Ms. Brown incorporated new literacies strategies and materials into practice in her classroom by engaging her students in the socio-cultural process of collecting information about themselves, using that information to project possible future outcomes, and then comparing their histories to those of well known African American figures. She integrated the use of technology as a mechanism for research, writing, illustration and distribution of student work.

By reenacting a historical slave tradition practiced in the south, Ms. Brown used a participatory process in helping her students make an association with their cultural past and to signify a new beginning (a possible clean slate for previous behavior and academic failure). Though, to some degree, this project might be considered an example of "old wine in new bottles," the use of a socio-cultural lens, the participatory aspects of the culminating activity, and the distributed nature of the students' work in sharing with others their findings and dreams for the future, signal a shift away from the traditional research project turned in only to the teacher and returned with a grade to one in which students are actively engaged in using their out-of-school experiences and history, paired with technology, to create new meaning. The impact of this project, and the resulting increase in student engagement, investment in learning, and academic performance while involved in the tasks, provides a glimpse into the potential new literacies may offer special education.

Conclusion

Educators working with students identified with mild disabilities already have many skills, strategies, and methods of intervening to meet the specific and unique needs of this population, including knowledge of technology and its use. These teachers work daily to motivate and engage learners who may be disenfranchised by their school-defined deficits in multiple areas of learning and literacy. New literacies offers another lens through which to view these learners and the provision of learning. It offers the combination of expanding the use of technology, including digital technologies, to increase students' in-school and out-of-school connectedness by using what is familiar to gain and hold student interest. It offers the idea of making the classroom one in which socio-cultural demands and needs are more fully considered when planning instruction. It offers a philosophy in which participation, collaboration, and distribution of shared ideas is planned for and promoted. For students who may be alienated, at-risk, below grade level in achievement, or lack skills in social interactions, implementing new literacy practices offers educators a means not only of creating engaging and meaningful lessons but also the opportunity to use advances in the digital world as tools for creating and communicating ideas within their social contexts.

References

Algozzine, B. & White, R. (2002). Preventing problem behaviors using school-wide discipline. In B. Algozzine and P. Kay (Eds.), *Preventing problem behaviors* (pp. 85-103). Thousand Oaks, CA: Corwin Press.

Alvermann, D. E. & Heron, A. H. (2001). Literacy identity work: Playing to learn with popular media. *Journal of Adolescent & Adult Literacy, 45*(2), 118-122.

Assistive Technology Act of 1998. Retrieved on October 26, 2008, from http://www.section508.gov

Attwood, T. (2008). An overview of autism spectrum disorders. In K. Dunn Burton and P. Wolfberg (Eds.), *Learners on the autism spectrum: Preparing highly qualified educators* (pp. 18-43). Shawnee Mission, KS: AAPC .

Bawden, D. (2008). Origins and concepts of digital literacy. In C. Lankshear & M. Knobel (Eds.), *Digital literacies: Concepts, policies, and practices* (pp.17-32). New York: Peter Lang.

Beirne-Smith, M., Patton, J. R. & Kim, S. H. (2006). *Mental retardation: An introduction to intellectual disabilities* (7th ed.). Upper Saddle River, NJ: Pearson.

Bender, W.N. (2008). *Learning disabilities: Characteristics, identification, and teaching strategies* (6th ed.). Boston: Allyn & Bacon.

Bitz, M. (2004). The Comic Book Project: Forging alternative pathways to literacy. *Journal of Adolescent & Adult Literacy, 47*(7), 574-586.

Boutout, E. A. (2006). What are autism spectrum disorders? In E.A. Boutout and M. Tincani (Eds.), *Autism spectrum disorders handouts: What parents need to know* (pp. 7-9). Austin, TX: PRO-ED.

Cosden, M., Brown, C. & Elliot, K. (2002). Development of self-understanding and self-esteem in children and adults with learning disabilities. In B.L. Wong and M.L. Donahue (Eds.)., *The social dimensions of learning disabilities: Essays in honor of Tanis Bryan* (pp. 33-51). Mahwah, NJ: Lawrence Erlbaum.

Curriculum Review (2004, September). Get students in on the comic-book writing act. *44*, 8-9.

Deschler, D. (2008). *SIMS.* Center for Research on Learning at the University of Kansas. Retrieved on October 22, 2008 from http://www.ku-crl.org/.

Edyburn, D.L. (2003). *What every teacher should know about assistive technology.* Boston, MA: Allyn & Bacon.

Elder-Hinshaw, R., Manset-Williamson, G., Nelson, J. M., & Dunn, M. W. (2006). Engaging older students with reading disabilities: Multimedia inquiry projects supported by reading assistive technology. *Teaching Exceptional Children, 39*, 6-11.

Elksnin, L. & Elksnin, H. (1993). A review of picture interest inventories: Implications for vocational assessment. *Journal of Psychoeducational Assessment,* 11, 323-336.

Ellis, E. (2004). *The makes sense strategies model.* Retrieved on October 29, 2008, from Masterminds Publishing at http://www.graphicorganizers.com/

Faraone, S.V., Beiderman, J., Monuteaux, M.C., Doyle, A.E., & Seidman, L.J. (2001). A psychometric measure of learning disability predicts educational failure four years later in boys with attention deficit/hyperactivity disorder. *Journal of Attention Disorders, 4,* 220-230.

Flavell, J. (1979). Metacognition and cognitive monitoring: A new area of cognitive-developmental inquiry. *American Psychologist, 34,* 906-911.

Forness, S. R. & Kavale, K.A. (2001). ADHD and a return to the medical modeled special education. *Education and Treatment of Children, 24,* 224-247.

Fuchs, L.S., Fuchs, D., Hamlett, C.L., & Appleton, A.C. (2002). Explicitly teaching for transfer: Effects on the mathematical problem-solving performance of students with learning disabilities. *Learning Disabilities Research and Practice, 17,* 90-106.

Gettinger, M., & Seibert, J.K. (2002). Contribution of study skills to academic competence. *School Psychology Review, 31,* 350-365.

Glaeser, B. C., Pierson, M. R., & Fritschmann, N. (2003). Comic strip conversations: A positive behavioral support strategy. *Teaching Exceptional Children, 36,* 14-19.

Golan, O. & Baron-Cohen, S. (2008). Systemizing emotions: Using interactive multimedia as a teaching tool. In K. Dunn Burton & P. Wolfberg (Eds.), *Learners on the autism spectrum: Preparing highly qualified educators* (pp. 234-253). Shawnee Mission, KS: AAPC.

Gray, C. (1994). *Comic strip conversations.* Arlington, TX: Future Horizons.

Hagood, M.C. (2007). Linking popular culture to literacy learning and teaching in the 21st century. In B. J. Guzzetti (Ed.), *Literacy for the new millennium: Adolescent literacy (Vol 3),* (pp.223-238). Westport, CT: Praeger.

Hagood, M.C. & Ash, G.E. (1999, April). *"I want my MTV" Reading fluency, student motivation, Karaoke, and pop culture: An exploration of repeated readings in an adolescent social context.* Paper presented at the American Educational Research Association, Montreal, Canada.

Hagood, M., Provost, M. C., Skinner, E., & Egelson, P. (2008). Teachers' and students' literacy performance in and engagement with new literacies strategies in underperforming middle schools. *Middle Grades Research Journal, 3,* 57-95.

Hardman, M.L., Drew, C.J., Egan, M.W. (2005). *Human exceptionality: School, community, and family* (8th ed.). New York: Allyn & Bacon.

Ito, M. (2008). *Participatory learning in a networked society:Lessons from the Digital Youth Project*. Presentation for the 2008 Annual Meeting of the American Educational Research Association Presidential session. Retrieved on February 12, 2009 from http://www.itofisher.com/mito/publications/partici patory_l.html

Ito, M., Horst, H., Bittanti, M., Boyd, D., Herr-Stephenson, B., Lange, P.G., Pascoe, C.J., Robinson, L., Baumer, S., Cody, R., Mahendran, D., Martinez, K., Perkel, D., Sims, C., & Tripp, L. (2008, November). *Living and learning with new media: Summary of findings from the Digital Youth Project*. Retrieved February 14, 2009 from http://digitalyouth.ischool.berkeley.edu

Laing, S. P. & Kamhi, A. G. (2002). The use of think-aloud protocols to compare inferencing abilities in average and below-average readers. *Journal of Learning Disabilities, 35*(5), 436-447.

Lankshear, C. & Knobel, M. (2006). *New literacies: Everyday practices & classroom learning*. Maidenhead, England: Open University Press.

Lankshear, C. & Knobel, M. (2007). Sampling the "new" in new literacies. In M. Knobel & C. Lankshear (Eds.), *A new literacies sampler* (pp.1-24). New York, NY: Peter Lang.

Lankshear, C. & Knobel, M. (2008). Introduction: Digital literacies— Concepts, policies, and practices. In Lankshear, C. & Knobel, M. (Eds.) *Digital literacies: Concepts, policies, and practices.* (pp.1-16). New York, NY: Peter Lang.

Lenz, B. K, Deshler, D. D., & Kissam, B. R. (2004). *Teaching content to all: Evidence-based inclusive practices in middle and secondary schools.* Boston: Pearson, Allyn & Bacon.

Little, E. (2006). Technology integration as an intervention strategy for at-risk eighth graders. *Meridian Middle School Computer Technologies Journal, 2*(9). Retrieved on September 12, 2008, from http://www.ncsu.edu/meridian/sum2006/tech_integration/index.htm

Martin, A. (2005). DigEuLit: A European framework for digital literacy: A progress report. Retrieved October 31, 2008, from http://www.jelit.org/65/01/JeLit_Paper_31.pdf.

Meltzer, L. (Ed.). (2007). *Executive function in education: From theory to practice.* New York: Guilford.

More, C. (2008). Digital stories targeting social skills for children with disabilities: Multidimensional learning. *Intervention in School and Clinic, 43*, 168-177.

Moreno, R., Mayer, R. E., Spires, H. A., & Lester, J. C. (2001). The case for social agency in computer-based teaching: Do students learn more deeply when they interact with animated pedagogical agents? *Cognition and Instruction, 19*, 177-213.

Myers, J. & Lytle, S. (1986). Assessment of the learning process. *Exceptional Children, 53*(2), 138-144.

O'Connor, R. E., White, A., & Swanson, H. L.(2007). Repeated reading versus continuous reading: Influences on reading fluency and comprehension. *Exceptional Children, 74*, 31-46.

Rasinski, T. (2004). Creating fluent readers. *Educational Leadership, 61*, 46-51.

Rehabilitation Act of 1973, amended 1998, Section 508 (29 U.S.C. 794d). Retrieved on October 26, 2008, from http://www.section508.gov

Riesland, E. (2005). Visual literacies in the classroom. *New horizons for learning.* Retrieved on October 30, 2008 from http://www.newhorizons.org/strategies/literacy/riesland.htm.

Robin, B.R. (2008). Digital storytelling: A powerful technology tool for the 21st century classroom. *Theory into Practice, 47*, 220-228.

Rogers, M. F. & Myles, B. S. (2001). Using social stories and comic strip conversations to interpret social situations for an adolescent with Asperger Syndrome. *Intervention in School and Clinic, 36*(5), 310-313.

Rucklidge, J.J. & Tannock, R. (2002). Neuropsychological profiles of adolescents with ADHD: Effects of reading difficulties and gender. *Journal of Child Psychology and Psychiatry and Allied Disciplines, 43*, 988-103.

Russell, J. (1997). *Autism as an executive disorder.* Oxford, UK: Oxford University Press.

Schwartz, A. & Rubinstein-Ávila, E. (2006). Understanding the manga hype: Uncovering the multimodality of comic book literacies. *Journal of Adolescent & Adult Literacy, 50*(1), 40-49.

Simpson, R. (2005). *Autism spectrum disorders: Interventions and treatments for children and youth.* Thousand Oaks, CA: Corwin Press.

Skinner, E. (2006—unpublished document). Literacy practices ethnography. *Professional Development Manual for the Center of Excellence for the Advancement of New Literacies in Middle Grades.* Charleston: College of Charleston.

Skinner, E.N. (2007). "Using movie trailers." Workshop conducted for teachers by the Center of Excellence for the Advancement of New Literacies in Middle Grades.

Skyler, A. Higgins, K., & Boone, R. (2007). Strategies for adapting WebQuests for students with learning disabilities. *Intervention in School and Clinic, 43*, 20-28.

Smith, S., Boone, R, & Higgins, K. (1998). Expanding the writing process to the web. *Teaching Exceptional Children, 30*, 22-26.

Therrien, W. J. & Hughes, C. (2008). Comparison of repeated reading and question generation on students' fluency and comprehension. *Learning Disabilities: A Contemporary Journal, 6*(1), 1-16.

Thomas, A. (2007). Blurring and breaking through the boundaries of narrative, literacy, and identity in adolescent fan fiction. In Knobel, M. & Lankshear, C. (Eds.) *A new literacies sampler* (pp.137-165). New York: Peter Lang.

U.S. Department of Education, Office of Special Education Programs. (2002). *Twenty-fourth annual report to Congress on the implementation of the Individuals with Disabilities Act.* Washington, DC: Author.

U.S. Department of Education. (2002). *No child left behind act.* Retrieved on January 20, 2009 from http://www.ed.gov/nclb.

U.S. Department of Education. (2004). *Individuals with disabilities educational improvement act.* Retrieved on October 26, 2008 from http://frwebgate.access.gpo.gov/cgi-bin/getdoc.cgi?dbname=108_cong_public_law&docid=f:publ446.108.

Vadasy, P. F. & Sanders, E. A. (2008). Benefits of repeated reading intervention for low-achieving fourth- and fifth-grade students. *Remedial and Special Education, 29*(4), 235-249.

Vaughn, S., Erlbaum, B. & Boardman, A.G. (2001). The social functioning of students with learning disabilities: Implications for inclusion. *Exceptionality, 9,* 47-66.

Winner, M. (2008). Social thinking: Cognition to enhance communication and learning. In K. Dunn Burton and P. Wolfberg (Eds.), *Learners on the autism spectrum: Preparing highly qualified educators* (pp. 208-233). Shawnee Mission, KS: AAPC

Suggestions for Readings in Mild Disabilities

Beirne-Smith, M., Patton, J. R. & Kim, S. H. (2006). *Mental retardation: An introduction to intellectual disabilities* (7th ed.). Upper Saddle River, NJ: Pearson.

Bender, W.N. (2008). *Learning disabilities: Characteristics, identification, and teaching strategies* (6th ed.). Boston: Pearson, Allyn, & Bacon.

Burton, K.D. & Wolfberg, P, (Eds.), (2008). *Learners on the autism spectrum: Preparing highly qualified educators.* Shawnee Mission, KS: AAPC.

Jordon, D.R. (2006). *Overcoming attention deficit disorder in children, adolescents, and adults* (4th ed.). Austin, TX: Pro-ED.

Hardnam, M.L., Drew, C.J., Egan, M.W. (2005). *Human exceptionality: School, community, and family* (8th ed.). New York: Allyn & Bacon.

Lenz, B. K, Deshler, D. D., & Kissam, B. R. (2004). *Teaching content to all: Evidence-based inclusive practices in middle and secondary schools.* Boston: Pearson, Allyn & Bacon.

CHAPTER NINE

Vignettes of Successful Middle School Teachers Who Use New Literacies

PAULA E. EGELSON

Introduction

> New literacies is a very powerful movement, and I walked into it after my first year of teaching. I was probably more receptive than some of the veteran teachers. I'm glad that I found new literacies early in my teaching career because I would hate to be left in the dust if I didn't know this stuff. (Gina, sixth grade social studies teacher)

This is the journey of four middle school teachers who successfully implemented new literacies in their classrooms. These four educators taught at two schools that took part in a two-year professional development initiative at their schools to implement new literacies strategies in their social studies and English/language arts classrooms. Teachers at both schools participated in several professional development institutes that included the theoretical underpinnings of new literacies, understanding of the Four Resources Model, introductory new literacies strategies, and such strategies as digital storytelling, blogging, and the use of *PhotoStory* and *Moviemaker* software to create student documentaries. Participating teachers also were in new literacies study groups during the school year several times a month. The study groups consisted of sixth, seventh, and eighth grade level social studies and language arts teachers and in some cases, special education teachers. They discussed new literacies strategies and classroom implementation.

Within this study, I employed a 21st century definition of reading that conceptualized literacy as socially situated and culturally constructed (Barton, Hamilton, & Ivanic, 2000) and of text to include both print and non-print texts that acknowledged the vast literacy competencies in adolescents' literacy repertoires. Out-of-school and in-school literacies were linked to assist teachers and middle school students in becoming better users of text in their 21st century world that advanced the understanding and implementation of new literacies teaching strategies for middle school teachers.

The definitions of new literacy for the teachers who are portrayed in this chapter were varied, but some similarities remained. Successful teacher implementers talked about expanding the traditional definition of literacy to include students' out-of-school culture and interests and using those strategies in the classroom for instructional purposes. For one successful new literacies teacher, it was all about incorporating new forms of technology into her classroom instruction. For another, new literacies was anything beyond opening a textbook and reading it.

My perspective on new literacies came from my own experiences as a middle school reading teacher in the Blue Ridge Mountains. I taught adolescent students living in poverty who struggled with reading. Our school was located in a small mill town past its prime, a place of little hope. I thought it was critical for my students to discover themselves and their talents in order to become academically motivated. Introducing their world into our classroom was one way to achieve that goal. Our classroom was filled with images and text of the time period—movie posters of the movies "Top Gun" and "Star Wars"; pictures of television and pop music stars Kirk Cameron, Justine Bateman, and Michael Jackson; and photos from the magazines *Tiger Beat*, *Jet*, and *Sports Illustrated*. Current popular literature—such as *The Outsiders* (Hinton, 1967) and *Old Yeller* (Gipson, 1965)—was read as a class. Students kept daily journals, and our intensive creative writing sessions focused on real topics in their lives. We created a monthly newspaper that focused on (gossipy) school news, and one comprehensive assignment compiled the history of our community school that involved interviewing community members. I realize now I was incorporating multiliteracies, a variety of texts, in my classroom. These were forms of communication that included cultural and linguistic diversity although my literacies remained print based. My students used these literacies to live and learn in a community of learners. Today I view new literacies as an avenue for student growth, both personally (in finding student voice) and academically (in achieving).

For me, the ideas surrounding new literacies have expanded my understanding of traditional literacy—reading, writing, listening, viewing, and speaking—over the past three years and incorporated students' out-of-school culture with the use of iPods, text messaging, blogs, comics, raps, graphic novels, and fanfiction into the school's instructional program.

Research Study

A total of 40 language arts, social studies, special education teachers and media specialists from two of the six middle schools (grades 6–8) participated in the larger study (Hagood, Provost, Skinner, & Egelson, 2008). Both schools served urban populations and were located in a mid-sized southeastern city. Demographically the schools were similar, but in some ways they differed from other middle schools in the district. The African American and Hispanic student populations were greater at the project schools, and students at the two project schools qualified for free and reduced-price lunch at a greater rate (see Table 9.1).

Table 9.1 School District Middle Schools

	New Literacies Project Schools (2)	Other Middle Schools in the District
Student Ethnicity	African American—74% Hispanic—5%	African American—43% Hispanic— 3%
Student Free/Reduced Lunch Rate	Free Lunch—65% Reduced Lunch—26%	Free Lunch— 44% Reduced Lunch—49%

This chapter presents findings of successful implementers of new literacies teaching in their English and/or social studies content areas. Specifically, data were analyzed to determine the attributes that characterized successful new literacies teacher implementers. Successful teachers in this study are those who (1) had a theoretical understanding of new literacies, (2) consistently and actively participated in new literacies professional development, (3) integrated new literacies into their classroom instruction on a regular basis, and (4) constructively reflected on new literacies successes and challenges.

Review of the Literature

The review of literature focuses on the fidelity of program implementation that is the adoption rather than the adaption of an initiative. In addition, teacher quality research is included. Specifically inputs of teacher quality such as certification and a bachelor's degree are addressed as well as teacher traits and classroom behavior.

An examination of teacher implementation research supported what we had informally observed in successful implementers of new literacies. The highest evaluations were in classrooms where teachers' procedural fidelity ratings were at the uppermost level (Maheady et al., 2004). The lowest evaluations were in classrooms where teachers *adapted* rather than *adopted* the procedures. Maheady's research signifies that teachers who adapted new literacies changed the strategies in some way; educators who adopted new literacies presented them in a precise manner. Programs were only as good as the quality of the implementation; when the quality varied, the outcomes were affected

(Gunn, 2005). This meant that inferior implementation equaled negative outcomes. In fact, research supported the theory that successful teacher program implementation was associated with teacher quality. The United States government, through the working of the No Child Left Behind legislation, has also noted the important relation between teacher quality and student success. The U.S. Department of Education defined highly qualified teachers as those individuals who hold a bachelor's degree, are fully certified, and demonstrate content knowledge in the core subjects they teach (Rand, 2007). These qualifications were described as inputs to teacher success. Linda Darling-Hammond (2000) followed a similar definition of teacher quality in her study on Teacher Quality and Student Achievement. She found that measures of teacher education and certification were the strongest correlates of student achievement in reading and mathematics.

Other researchers have developed domains of teacher quality that focus on teachers' inputs and their work in the classroom. They included such categories as teacher as a person, classroom management and organization, organizing for instruction, implementing instruction, monitoring student progress, and potential (Stronge, 2003). Furthermore, Kennedy (2008) proposed three broad groupings of teacher qualities: personal resources, teacher performance, and effectiveness. Some researchers have recently clustered desirable and effective teaching traits to predict teacher effectiveness, rather than isolated traits. For example, Rockoff, Jacob, Kane, and Staiger (2008) reported that predictors of teacher effectiveness included teaching specific content knowledge, cognitive ability, personality traits such as conscientiousness and extroversion, feelings of self-efficacy, and scores on a prescreening test. Study participants were New York City first-year teachers (2006–2007). None of these traits on their own was statistically significant, but clustered together these measures represented/determined teacher quality.

Successful New Literacies Teacher Implementers

The four successful new literacies teachers described in this chapter were nominated by their peers to present their outstanding new literacies work at an international reading conference preconvention institute. In all, six teachers—three from each new literacies project school—were nominated and presented at the conference workshop. For the purposes of this chapter, the vignettes of four high-implementing teachers (all names are pseudonyms) are presented.

All of the nominated teachers—Bill, Gloria, Gina, and Lynn—are graduates of various southeastern colleges and universities and began implementing new literacies after attending the first of four, two-day new literacies professional development institutes that were part of the larger study. They did not delay. Although the selected teachers shared some similar qualities, each teacher was unique in his or her own way. They represented a cross-section of teachers in their southeastern urban school district. Background information about the four teachers is found in Table 9.2.

Not surprisingly, the selected teachers said they benefited from new literacies in a variety of ways. For Bill it was being introduced to new ways of teaching the social studies content, while for Gloria it was the exposure to cutting-edge technology. Gina said it was an eye-opener for her that she could go beyond the textbook as a primary tool of instruction, while Lynn said that new literacies participation represented the introduction of good instructional strategies.

Table 9.2 Facts about Successful New Literacies Teacher Implementers

	New to the Profession (0 to 5 years' experience)	Second Profession	Master's Degree	Subjects Taught
Bill, white male, mid 20s	✓			Social Studies
Gloria, African American, late 50s			✓	Reading
Gina, white, late 20s	✓	✓		Language Arts and Social Studies
Lynn, white, late 20s	✓		✓	Language Arts

In the following four sections, vignettes of each teacher are presented. These vignettes provide teacher reflections about new literacies (both their individual and schoolwide implementation), about their linking of new literacies strategies to state content standards, about their perceived successes and failures, and information about their presentations at the international conference. Data were analyzed from interviews, conference presentations, teacher and student new literacies artifacts of classroom instruction, and classroom and study group observations by the researchers.

Specifically, the teachers were rated over a two-year period on Freebody and Luke's Four Resources Model (1990). The model emphasized the various capabilities that literacy involved across contexts and the change of literacy activities from place to place. The Model proposed a range of literacy practices that included Code Breaker (decoding—How do I crack this code?); Text User (comprehending—What does this mean to me?); Text User (using texts functionally—What do I do with this text?); and, Text Analyst (critically analyzing and transforming text—What does this text do to me?) It was critical that literate students needed to employ and mix all of these Freebody and Luke textual resources in the 21st century.

The second observation instrument was the Team Meeting Observation Form rubric (adapted from Westheimer, 1998) that included components of study group meetings where new literacies strategies were discussed. Areas such as group responsibilities, participation, instruction, new literacies use, decision-making and collegiality were included as a part of the instrument.

Participating teachers were asked to create at least one unit of study per semester. A unit of study included specific content goals and objectives, corresponding state content standards, and the inclusion of a new literacies strategy. The four successful teachers were very aware of the content they needed to cover in the units of study. Teachers made explicit connections between standards and new literacies strategies and developed scoring rubrics for assessments. They also held high student achievement expectations and strived to make their instruction relevant and motivational for their students. Most of the new literacies strategies these teachers used incorporated technology, were hands on, and required students to create new text. For example, gifted and talented students at one school created movie trailers that depicted several battles from the Civil War. In a sixth grade classroom, students created MySpace pages for Roman leaders. (MySpace is a social networking site that appeals to teens.)

Note at the beginning of each vignette how each teacher defined text. Bill had a broad and open-ended meaning, while Gloria's definition was traditional and more tightly defined. Given the individuals, the text definitions they offered were not surprising. Bill was young, savvy with technology, and embraced new literacies from the very beginning. Gloria was a veteran teacher who initially saw new literacies as an add-on and something that represented technology use. Lynn and Gina's definitions of new literacies were especially surprising. Lynn was someone who had been implementing new literacies before she had a name for it, yet her definition of text was confined and narrowly defined. Gina's defined text as traditional print, yet the new literacies strategies she implemented in her classroom were beyond that.

Bill—"Text is almost anything you can get meaning from"

Teaching social studies is Bill's passion. He has been a sixth grade social studies teacher for several years and has a supportive group of colleagues at his middle school. All the social studies teachers at his school like teaching, continually push the envelope and attempt new instructional strategies, and enjoy trying out the latest technologies. They really want to engage their students in learning. The yearly state social studies scores at Bill's school are the highest of all the core content areas at their school. Bill sees new literacies as going beyond traditional reading and writing. He believes that new literacies involves examining other literacies that teachers are capable of working with. For example, as a social studies teacher, Bill found that new literacies allowed him to familiarize students with social studies information in new ways and got them excited about learning the information. This reflected his definition of new literacies. The strategies were "out of the box" for him and he saw that as a good thing.

Bill has used new literacies to teach social studies content rather than literacy; he has found the new literacies resources to be very helpful. They fit with his style of teaching. When his class did a unit on creating comics that centered on Early Man, he pulled in language arts and incorporated story elements into his instruction. Besides using comics with new literacies, Ben used the free software *Photo Story* to have students create historic Roman documentaries, and he implemented an art in history project (students creating relics) that reflected a new literacies influence. He found new literacies implementation to be time consuming ("pretty involved") because of the necessity of covering all the content standards. Bill remarked that teaching in a low-performing school also put extra pressure on teachers to succeed with their students.

Bill participated in some of the grade level, bi-monthly new literacies study groups at his school over the two-year period. Although his study group was moderately collegial and participated in discussions on new literacies, the group never became fully functional because study group members did not take responsibility for group tasks (such as meeting facilitation, note taking, timing, or agenda setting) nor made decisions as a group. The group felt that it was easier to implement new literacies in social studies rather than language arts/reading because of the focus on content.

Bill completed two comprehensive units of study in a year's time that incorporated new literacies. The first was an Early Man comic strip that was taken from a chapter in the social studies text. The unit included incorporating social studies content and story elements into a comic strip. Students were to show that Early Man moved from being nomads (hunters and gathers) to building communities and becoming farmers. Bill asked students to create four characters (could be students in the classroom), and create a title, an introduction, some type of conflict, a resolution, and a conclusion. Students were asked to create 24 comic strip slides in total. Bill provided students with comic strip examples. He also made accommodations for English language learners in the classroom. (Bill's notes were translated into Spanish and the ELL students were able to draw comics and understand the concepts.) Students in his class were very successful with this assignment and grasped and emphasized the grade-level standards including concepts of irrigation, domesticated animals, and working as a group in the fields in their comic strips.

Bill also completed an extensive unit on the ancient Roman Empire using *Photo Story*, a free program that is downloaded from the internet. *Photo Story* is used to create digital stories using photographs. The standard covered in this unit of study was summarizing the significant political and cultural features of classical Roman civilization. Students were directed to individually use *Photo Story* to document ancient Roman architecture, roads, arches, keystones, and aqueducts using a visual format. Students gathered photos from websites and imported the pictures into the *Photo Story* program. They created titles for the photos and added motion, their voices, and (popular) music, thus creating their own text. Once again, the English language learners were able to fully participate in this activity because of Bill's accommodations. For example, the directions were translated into Spanish for the students. *Photo Story* documentaries were shared with the class and worked as an introduction to the unit on ancient Rome. Bill's rubric for students included the quality of photos, captions, and narration. He says next time he teaches the unit, he will incorporate *Photo Story* activities at the conclusion of the unit of study rather than at the beginning. Students can then learn content before creating the documentaries. Bill commented that the students required lots of assistance in completing the *Photo Story* project and that the amount of time required for intensive technology-driven projects was extensive. Bill thought that new literacies opened up a variety of ways for students to receive information and to get them excited about the content. Their level of engagement really increased and it was easier to keep them on task.

Gloria—"Text is written or printed material that forms the main body of a publication"

Gloria is a sixth- through eighth- grade reading teacher with 37 years of experience teaching middle school and high school students. She is viewed as the "go-to" person in her school because of her experience and understanding of struggling students. Gloria deeply cares about the students in her school and keeps a positive attitude. Her attitudes about new literacies center on her increased exposure to technology during the two years of professional development. She sees new literacies as redefining literacy because of the emphasis on technology and its ever-changing presence. For Gloria, new literacies represents learning about new technologies (e.g., blogging, wikis, texting) and strategies for implementing these technologies into her instruction. She also views new literacies as an opportunity to experiment with instruction.

Gloria was part of a new literacies study group that struggled. Often Gloria was not able to attend the study group because of her literacy coach responsibilities (another role she played in her school). The group participated in discussions about new literacies, made decisions as a group, and displayed a moderate level of collegiality (e.g., teachers talked about new literacy strategies but did not work together in implementing them).

Gloria worked with the struggling, reluctant readers in her school. Many of her students experienced family problems. She used bibliotherapy as a way to reach these low-performing students. In a unit of study she devoted to new literacies, Gloria used a popular culture story of teenager with a troubled family to share with her students. The use of a videocamera was the key new literacies element. Gloria used this story with her students to teach higher thinking skills and to integrate reading, writing, speaking, listening, and viewing. Ironically Gloria's unit of study did not include a major technology component. The state standards that supported Gloria's unit included accessing, reading, comprehending, and using information from a variety of sources, using word analysis and vocabulary strategies to read fluently, analyzing literary text, and examining the effect of the author's craft. Gloria used all four levels of Freebody and Luke's Four Resources Model—Code Breaker (decoding, students were expected to pronounce key vocabulary words), Text Participant (comprehension, students predicted what was going to happen in the story), Text User (creating new text, students wrote a script based on the text), and Text Analyst (analyzing text, students videotaped their dialogue). The students read the short story, predicted what was going to happen, confirmed their predictions, wrote a script, and videotaped their work. The work samples included videotaped interviews and the development of group scripts. Gloria created a rubric that included level of group participation, quality of the script, and quality of the videotaped interview. Gloria found that 100 percent of her students participated; they collaborated in small groups; the activity challenged the students' learning styles; and it was an extension of learning beyond the textbook. Gloria noted that her students were definitely more engaged with new literacies activities.

Gina—"Text is anything that is written, typed, or published, but it doesn't necessarily have to be a page that you can physically put your hands on. It can be a page on the internet"

Gina started out working in the business world, but she wanted to make a difference in children's lives, so she went back to school to become a middle school teacher. She has a wonderful rapport with her students and a good sense of humor. Gina was open to the concept of new literacies from the beginning. She was also enthusiastic, opening up her classroom to observers and being an advocate for the new literacies professional development at her school. For her, new literacies is anything that is beyond a textbook. She sees it as looking at a cartoon, a comic strip, viewing a video or a movie trailer. Students can apply their knowledge and create something new using modern media. What revolutionalized Gina about new literacies was the notion that a teacher could go beyond the textbook in teaching subject matter. She began to see the textbook as being overused, and not a necessary tool for teaching. New literacies was a creative approach for her, one that made learning fun and positive for students.

Gina is both a sixth grade language arts and a social studies teacher, and she found it easier to incorporate new literacies strategies in her social studies lessons during the first year of implementation. She thought implementation was easier because of a focus on historical figures in social studies that complemented new literacies strategies. During the first year, selected teachers and students on her team developed movie trailers of Alexander the Great, cartoon strips of the Fly Boys, and participated in social studies storytelling through raps and cartoons. Gina thought that teachers "kind of blocked" on language arts initially and had a difficult time implementing new literacies strategies into their instruction but resolved it during the second year of implementation. During the second year, Gina's students created MySpace pages from characters in books and developed comics or storyboards related to the story plots from outstanding adolescent literature.

Gina remarked, "There was initially hesitation on the part of the faculty in implementing new literacies strategies." She also commented that, "Other teachers were worried about losing control of their classrooms. They would be stepping away from the norm, and they didn't think the strategies would work...but they did!"

Teachers soon realized when they had a problem with a strategy that they usually needed to narrow the focus and provide implementation steps for students. Examples included using fewer vocabulary words with the raps and focusing on one or two historical figures rather than 10 or 11 when creating comics or storyboards.

Gina's new literacies study group was collegial, although leadership within the group was uneven. (Sometimes there was a group leader and a scribe, and sometimes not.) The teachers participated in the discussion and contributed, but it was difficult for them to make decisions because they had so many ideas. The whole group agreed that their sixth graders' reading levels ranged from third grade to seventh grade. For many students fluency was lacking as were decoding skills, and students did not write in complete sentences. Gina and her team members also found the sixth grade students to be somewhat immature, argumentative, and sensitive.

Her openness to new literacies was reflected in the myriad of new literacies strategies Gina employed in her classroom. Gina incorporated the development of raps as a new literacies strategy with her students when they studied Egypt. The purpose of the raps was to improve fluency and understanding of key concepts. She provided examples of raps to the students and then asked them to create, memorize, and perform their own rap. Gina also created a complicated (in her own words) scoring rubric. What she found was that students were unable to successfully complete the assignment. She realized later it was an open-ended task that required too much time and a higher level of thinking. Gina found that the honors students, who travel as a cohort to all their classes, were better able to tackle the assignment and create the first couple of lines of the raps. She also realized that the assignment was somewhat abstract. Students in her other classes were not even able to start the task. Gina found that if she provided a completed rap to students and asked them to expand on it, memorize it, respond to questions, and perform it, they were much more successful because the steps were more concrete. She also simplified the rubric, concentrating on one critical area: fluency. It became a performance-based assessment because students presented their raps to the rest of the class and they were scored by the teacher.

During the second year of the study, Gina incorporated a MySpace activity with her social studies unit on the Roman Empire. The social studies standard addressed the expansion and decline of the Roman Empire, including the reasons for its growth, the role of Caesar and Augustus, and weaknesses and threats that contributed to its downfall. Gina used a version of MySpace on paper (see Figure 9.1) as a way for students to learn content. She said the students saw the activity as very motivating and something they could relate to. Gina created a rubric that included the quality of student writing. Students selected one of five Roman leaders—Augustus, Caligula, Claudius, Nero, and Marcus Aurelius—and created a MySpace entry for them. Students responded to a series of questions using internet research as they created their MySpace pages. They also created a bibliography and an essay about their person's life and the impact on the Roman Empire.

Figure 9.1 Student Examples of MySpace

Gina also created a poetry unit incorporating MySpace. The English standards include understanding the characteristics of poetry and drama; clarifying the research topic; using direct quotations, paraphrasing and summarizing to incorporate into written works; and creating a list of sources. She developed a rubric for writing and expectations. Students were asked to choose a poem from the textbook that they enjoyed and research the author. They analyzed the poem, found the poetic elements in each poem, and created a MySpace paper version of the poet.

Gina is a highly creative teacher and after the pressure of the yearly state testing was completed, she tried a series of new literacies ideas with her students. "Rapping Grammar" and Grammar Girls podcasts were quite popular and effective with her students, and she used junk mail and newspapers to create comics based on adolescent literature such as *The Sisterhood of the Traveling Pants* (Brashares, 2001) and *The Rose that Grew from Concrete* (Shakur, 1999). Gina differentiated instruction by gender with popular adolescent literature; students created storyboards, another new literacies strategy, to denote the story elements. The songs of Bob Marley, and the movie clips from "Prince of Egypt," "The Darjeeling Express," and "Bill and Ted's Excellent Adventure" were used with corresponding social studies chapters where students created their own text. Censorship continued to be an issue with the use of comics, lyrics, and movies Gina found; she closely examined materials before she presented them to students. She commented that new literacies really gave teachers options, and she found the strategies to be particularly helpful with her struggling students. Gina believed that new literacies had a big effect and a positive impact on the students. They were quite excited about participating in the activities and were definitely engaged. She also believed her students learned more quickly and absorbed more content when using new literacies.

Lynn—"Text is something you read. It applies to writing and communication"

Lynn came to the new literacies project with a strong background in technology, literature, and a willingness to try new things. In fact, she was already using new literacies strategies in her language arts classes and did not realize it. A real believer in the middle school concept (i.e. a focus on students' academic, emotional, and physical health; strong teacher team collaboration), she was a middle school team leader at her school and taught honors classes to seventh graders.

Lynn perceived new literacies as literacy outside the classroom based on children's interests brought into the classroom. She saw new ideas as the greatest gain in her involvement with new literacies. This view of new literacies fit with where Lynn was in the implementation process, beyond a beginner. Lynn initially experienced frustration with the new literacies implementation process. "At the beginning I was upset. Expectations were confusing. They weren't defined." She wasn't sure how she was supposed to implement new literacies as a member of a team. Lynn's frustration diminished over time as expectations became clearer and she became one of new literacies' biggest advocates.

Lynn's new literacies study group had its ups and downs at the beginning of the school year. There was some resentment within the group that some teachers worked harder than others, and that high-striving teachers did not want to share their ideas with the rest of the group. In addition, some of the teachers wanted to be assigned different content areas by the principal and this created group tension. Lynn was responsible for teaching honors language arts and felt initially that what she did in the classroom would not translate into other classes. The group eventually settled down and began to discuss new literacies strategies in depth. They came to consensus about decisions related to new literacies and ultimately generated a feeling of collegiality. There was a lack of leadership within the group, however; the same teacher consistently took responsibility for leading the group.

Lynn remarked that her seventh-grade students connected to "home text" and struggled with "school text." She thought it was a plus to use an iPod as a tool in creating new literacies strategies. It attracted positive attention from students because it was technology that was normally used outside the school walls. Lynn used iPods to enhance the curriculum and to increase attention and comprehension. It was the application of students' out-of-school literacies that complemented the students' traditional comprehension foundation. Lynn used a variety of iPod features—movies, television shows, audiobooks, podcasts, iTunes—to teach the elements of short stories, English mechanics, and writing dialogue. She also served as the unofficial iPod tutor to other teachers in her school.

Lynn was a whiz at incorporating movie themes when discussing story elements with students. "Belle" from "Beauty and The Beast" was used as an introduction to short stories, and the theme from "Armageddon" was incorporated to introduce plot. Michael Jackson's songs "Beat It" and "Man in the Mirror" supported point of view. Lynn's unit on propaganda centered on the documentary "Fast Food Nation." She pulled in corresponding songs, Superbowl commercials, and movie clips.

She found—like the other teachers—that she had to censure the materials she used with middle school students. Lynn was a believer in literature circles and had introduced graphic novels and mangas to her students using that approach. It took her awhile to figure out the mangas. They seemed so random to her and there was seemingly no character development. Lynn was definitely a "new idea" person, and she continuously thought of ways to introduce concepts and/or to reinforce a standard. Lynn felt there was engagement by students when using new literacies and that there might have been some increase in student achievement.

Results

Over the two years, I found that the teachers successful at implementing new literacies—integrating new literacies strategies with fidelity and consistently in their classrooms—were more effective teachers, and they also had better student results as compared to other participants. Based on observations, these results included more highly motivated students who wanted to do well academically; students who retained content knowledge at a greater rate; and students who performed better on classroom assessments.

The four teachers and their colleagues faced challenges in implementing new literacies in their respective schools. They included competing demands on their time, constantly changing school schedules, and a high-stakes state testing program. The four teachers overcame these obstacles by making new literacies a priority, implementing it with fidelity, and integrating it seamlessly into instruction.

Some of the teachers' work was not new literacies, but they implemented new literacies as best they could. As mentioned earlier, there were a variety of constraints that were both school related and self-imposed. And, based on their definitions of text and new literacies, the teachers' fortitude to implement new ideas resulted in changes in content coverage that invigorated teachers and motivated students.

The four successful new literacies teachers differed in race, background, age, gender, and years of teaching experience. In observing the actions and work of Bill, Gloria, Gina, and Lynn, they implemented new literacies with fidelity (Maheady et al., 2004). This meant they adopted rather than adapted new literacy strategies. The teachers also reflected the traits of successful teachers—cognitive ability, knowledge of subject matter, personality traits such as conscientiousness and extrovertism, and self-efficacy (Rockoff, Jacob, Kane, & Staiger, 2008). Not surprisingly, they shared many attributes that contributed to their new literacies success. The four teachers were highly dedicated to the teaching profession; they were highly committed to and knowledgeable in their content area(s); they were willing to experiment and to take risks; they wanted to collaborate and share ideas with peers; they were good communicators; they were supportive of students; and, they were continual learners.

In addition, they believed that their engagement with new literacies technology/techniques (blogging, iPods, texting, wikis, and podcasts) was a critical component of the professional development; they reported that participation in new literacies made them feel more confident as teachers; and they stated individually that student motivation, engagement, and attendance all increased due to new literacies. The teachers shared some concerns about new literacies. They were related to a lack of time during the school day to participate in new literacies meetings and projects. These teachers remarked that uninterested teachers in their respective schools pulled down the overall quality and impact of new literacies. Newer teachers initially worried about maintaining classroom discipline when implementing the new literacies strategies. This fear was unfounded.

Summary

Bill, Gloria, Gina, and Lynn, all high-quality teachers, represented a cross-section of educators in their district as far as race, age, teaching experience, gender, middle school grade/subject assignment, and training were concerned. These successful teacher implementers shared such attributes as dedication, intelligence, risk taking and collegiality, yet they defined new literacies differently, implemented it differently, and benefited from the professional development in different ways. They all successfully implemented new literacies that resulted in positive student outcomes. These teachers had the determination, vision, fortitude, and skill to make it happen in their schools. The new literacies project at these two middle schools resulted in a teacher-driven implementation supported by quality teachers with common attributes.

> I think new literacies has given me insight into what children want to learn, what is going to get them excited and encourage them to read and write more, instead of [doing] the basics. For example with the poetry project we are working on, a lot of them have gone over the top with the MySpace pages and their research...I think they go an extra mile sometimes with new literacies to find out more about things...I am definitely a better teacher because of new literacies. (Gina, sixth grade social studies teacher)

References

Barton, D., Hamilton, M., & Ivanic, R. (Eds.). (2000). *Situated literacies: Reading and writing in context.* New York: Routledge.

Brashares, A. (2001). *Sisterhood of the traveling pants.* New York: Random House Children's Books.

Darling-Hammond, L. (2000). Teacher quality and student achievement: A review of state policy evidence. *Education Policy Analysis Archives, 8*(1), 1–2.

Freebody, P., & Luke, A. (1990). Literacies programs: Debates and demands in cultural context. *Prospect: Australian Journal of TESOL, 5*(7), 7–16.

Gipson, F., (1965). *Old yeller.* New York: Scholastic Book Services.

Gunn, B. (2005). *Fidelity of implementation.* PowerPoint presented at the Oregon Institute of Research, Portland, OR.

Hagood, M. C., Provost, M., Skinner, E., & Egelson, P. (2008). Teachers' and students' literacy performance in and engagement with new literacies strategies in underperforming middle schools. *Middle Grades Research Journal 3*(3), 57–76.

Hinton, S. E. (1967). *The outsiders.* New York: Viking Press.

Kennedy, M. (2008). Sorting out teacher quality. *Phi Beta Kappa.* Retrieved October 23, 2008, fromhttp://find.galegroup.com.nuncio.cofc.edu/itx/retrieve.do?

Maheady, L., Harper, G., Mallette, B., & Karners, M. (2004). Preparing preservice teachers to implement classwide peer tutoring. *Teacher Education and Special Education, 27*(4), 408.

Rand (2007). Evaluating teacher quality under No Child Left Behind. *Research Brief.* Santa Monica, CA: Author.

Rockoff, J., Jacob, B., Kane, T., & Staiger, D. (2008). *Can you recognize an effective teacher when you recruit one?* Cambridge, MA: National Bureau of Economic Research.

Shakur, T. (1999). *The rose that grew from concrete.* New York: Simon and Schuster.

Skinner, E., Egelson, P., Hagood, M., & Provost, M. (2008, April). *Year two new literacies results.* Paper presented at the American Education Research Association. New York, NY.

Stronge, J. (2003). Hiring the best teachers. *Educational Leadership, 60,* Retrieved December 15, 2008, from http:web.ebscohost.com.nuncio.cofc.edu/ehost/pdf?vid=3&hid=21&sid=5fba6e2c-b7f9-40f9-8d29-3748ca840600%40sessionmgr8.

Westheimer, J. (1998). *Among schoolteachers: Community, autonomy and ideology in teacher's work.* New York: Teachers College Press.

About the Authors

Andrea M. Babkie, Ed.D., is a freelance writer and editor who has taught in the area of Special Education at several different universities.

Michael Bitz is the founder of the Comic Book Project (www.ComicBookProject.org) and co-founder of the Youth Music Exchange (www.YouthMusicExchange.org). He is the inaugural fellow in educational entrepreneurship at the Mind Trust in Indianapolis, and he is the recipient of the Union Square Arts Award for Social Justice and the Distinguished Alumni Early Career Award from Teachers College, Columbia University.

A. Jonathan Eakle is Associate Professor and Reading Program Director in the Johns Hopkins University School of Education. His research addresses multiple literacies in classrooms and out-of-school settings, creativity, and museum practices. Eakle teaches cross-cultural studies and clinical practicum. His work appears in *Reading Research Quarterly*, *Reading Teacher*, *Reading Online*, and other venues. Eakle is an editor of literacy publications and his co-edited book *Secondary School Literacy: What Research Reveals for Classroom Practice* was recently published by the National Council of Teachers of English.

Paula E. Egelson is the director of the Center for Partnerships to Improve Education at the College of Charleston (SC). The Center for Partnerships works with low-performing schools in South Carolina to improve student outcomes. She is also the co-director of the Center of Excellence for the Advancement of New Literacies in Middle Grades. Dr. Egelson has a background in research and is a former elementary and middle school teacher. She has developed teacher evaluation, literacy, high school performance assessment, class-size reduction, school improvement, and English language learners products for PreK-12 educators.

Barbara J. Guzzetti is a Professor in the Mary Lou Fulton College of Education, Division of Curriculum and Instruction at Arizona State University. She is also an affiliated faculty member in the College of Liberal Arts and Sciences in Women's and Gender Studies. Her current research and teaching interests center on adolescents' new literacies, particularly technoliteracies, and social justice and gender issues in literacy development and practice.

Margaret C. Hagood is Associate Professor of Literacy Education at the College of Charleston. She teaches undergraduate and graduate courses in early childhood, elementary, and middle grade literacies, focusing on sociocultural and poststructural theories relevant to new literacies. She is the Director of Research for the Center of the Advancement of New Literacies in Middle Grades, studying how middle grades educators and students understand and utilize new literacies to improve their literacy performance in teaching and learning in school. Her work appears in *Reading Research Quarterly*, *Language Arts*, *The Reading Matrix*, among others. She has recently coauthored *Connecting Texts and Texts That Connect: Pop Culture in the Classroom* with Donna Alvermann and Alison Heron-Hruby.

Amy Suzanne Johnson is an Assistant Professor in Language and Literacy in the Department of Instruction and Teacher Education at the University of South Carolina. She teaches literacy methods and assessment courses for undergraduate and graduate students. Amy researches how individuals extend their literacy practices across their life spans.

Melanie J. Lichtenstein is a teacher of the gifted and talented at a middle school in North Charleston, South Carolina, where she builds her student-centered curriculum around new literacies and social action. Melanie has explored new literacies in the classroom through process drama, creative writing and expression, and social action. Melanie's main area of interests lies in multicultural gifted education and student empowerment, and how to use new literacies to engage and empower culturally and linguistically diverse students.

Mary C. Provost is an Assistant Professor of Special Education and the Co-Director of the Center of Excellence for the Advancement of New Literacies in Middle Grades at the College of Charleston. Her research interests include staff development, response to intervention techniques, literacy and inclusive practices for students with mild to severe disabilities.

Achariya Tanya Rezak is a graduate student in Language and Literacy Education at the University of Georgia. Her interests focus on student use of online spaces to learn multiple literacies, particularly on manga scanlation, online communities of practice in LiveJournal, and technological multimodality in classroom instruction. She teaches courses in reading comprehension to middle school preservice teachers.

Jennifer Rowsell is an Assistant Professor of Literacy Education at Rutgers Graduate School of Education. Dr. Rowsell conducts research and writes in the areas of multimodality, New Literacy Studies, and family literacy. She is currently involved in three research studies: one looking at bridging the gap between student life worlds and school literacy; one looking at parents' circulation of information about children's literacy and development with Drs. Sue Nichols and Helen Nixon at the University of South Australia; and, another study looking at the production of new media and digital technologies with Dr. Mary P. Sheridan-Rabideau at the University of Wyoming.

Emily N. Skinner is an Assistant Professor in the Department of Teacher Education in the School of Education, Health and Human Development at the College of Charleston. Emily teaches literacy development and literacy methods courses for undergraduate and graduate students preparing to teach in preK-8th grade contexts. Emily is a principal investigator and the director of professional development for the Center for the Advancement of New Literacies in Middle Grades, a grant collaboration between the College of Charleston and the South Carolina Commission of Higher Education. The Center's work is focused on providing professional development and engaging in research related to middle school teachers' implementation of new literacies strategies in their classrooms.

Melissa I. Venters is a middle/high school certified teacher and has been teaching public school in Charleston, South Carolina, for three years. Her teaching experience includes eighth grade South Carolina History in the areas of inclusion, general, and honors levels; she currently teaches AP Government and Economics at the twelfth-grade level. She received her Bachelor of Arts in History from the College of Charleston and is currently working on her Master in Teaching Social Studies from Columbia University Teachers College.

AUTHOR INDEX

SUBJECT INDEX